NINETEEN YEARS CAPTIVITY IN THE HIGHLANDS OF CEYLON

NINETEEN YEARS
CAPTIVITY
IN THE
HIGHLANDS OF CEYLON

March 1660 - October 1679

ROBERT KNOX

From the Original Edition of
AN HISTORICAL RELATIONS, EDN, 1681

GYAN

Published by

Gyan Publishing House
5, Ansari Road
Daryaganj, New Delhi-110002
Phone: 011-47034999, 9811692060
E-mail: books@gyanbooks.com

Distribution Network
gyanbooks.com
India, USA, Canada, UK, Australia, France

ISBN : 978-81-212-3821-2 (PB)
First Published, Westminster 1903

2nd Impression 2020

Printed at: Gyan Press, Delhi.

Nineteen Years
Captivity in the Highlands of Ceylon
Author: Robert Knox

NINETEEN YEARS'

CAPTIVITY

IN THE

KINGDOM OF CONDE UDA

IN THE

Highlands of Ceylon,

SUSTAINED BY

CAPTAIN ROBERT KNOX;

BETWEEN

March 1660 & *October* 1679:

Together with his

SINGULAR DELIVERANCE

FROM THAT

STRANGE AND PAGAN LAND.

[From *An Historical Relation* &c., 1681. fol.]

INTRODUCTION TO VOLUME II

THE second volume of these travels opens with an abridgment of the first part of the celebrated *Itinerario* of Jan Huygen van Linschoten—'John the son of Hugh,' from the village of Linschoten in Utrecht, the probable home of his forefathers, but not his own birthplace. The author was born at Haarlem in or about 1563; in 1573, either before or just after the great siege of Haarlem, by the Duke of Alva, the family removed to Enkhuizen in North Holland, a town which escaped the Spanish re-conquest. At the age of sixteen, on December 6, 1576, young Jan started on his travels, and his first objective was remarkable. It was the country with which his countrymen, and especially the city of Enkhuizen and the province of North Holland, were so desperately struggling. Political war co-existed with an active commerce, and Linschoten sailed from the Texel in a fleet of some eighty vessels, bound for San Lucar in Andalusia. After a stay of six years in Spain (as the narrative tells us), mainly in Seville and Lisbon, Jan sought employment in the East Indian fleet, like his half-brother Willem Tin, who went in the same ship as *schrevijn* or *clerk* (not *purser*, as in the English translation, vol. ii. p. 7, etc.). Shortly after Linschoten's arrival at Goa, on September 21, 1583, John Newberie, Ralph Fitch, William Leedes, and James Storey were brought there under arrest from Ormuz, accused of being spies in the pay of Don Antonio, pretender to the crown of Portugal.[1] Drake's voyages in the Pacific and East

[1] For Linschoten's account of this, see vol. i. pp. 324-30.

Indies were of recent occurrence, and Englishmen were now regarded as somewhat of a dubious blessing in the Portuguese East. It was therefore with difficulty that Linschoten, his friend and comrade Bernard Burcherts of Hamburg, and Thomas Stevens the Jesuit, procured the release of Newberie, Fitch, and the other Englishmen. In 1584 Burcherts returned to Europe by the Persian Gulf, the Euphrates, and Aleppo; but Linschoten remained, hoping vainly for an opportunity of extending his travels to Eastern Asia. China and Japan, he wrote to his parents, were about the same distance as Portugal from the Malabar coast, a three years' journey: a Dutch friend of Linschoten's, one Dirck Gerritsz, had just been to the Far East as a gunner, and had pressed him to go too. In those distant and favoured lands two hundred ducats might easily be turned into six or seven hundred; but the necessary capital was wanting. Gerritsz, nicknamed 'the Chinaman' from his China voyages, was born at Enkhuizen, and spent in all twenty-six years in the Indies. He returned in the same ship with Linschoten, which sailed from Cochin on January 20, 1589; and from him comes most of the information of the *Itinerario* about the navigation of the China seas. In 1598 he piloted the Dutch fleet on its first voyage by the South-West Passage (of Magellan's Straits) to India. His notes on India are occasionally embedded in Linschoten; but their only proper edition was in Lucas Jansz Waghenaer's *Thresoor der Zeevaert* (Leyden, 1592). The *Itinerario* of Linschoten, as we have suggested, contains the results, not only of Linschoten's own experience, but of that of many other travellers; and the author, it is clear, was a collector of Hakluytian industry and judgment. He appears to have been hard at work upon it from the time of his return to Enkhuizen (September 3,

1592) until the complete publication of this encyclopædic survey of 'Cape Commerce' and 'Cape Routes' in the beginning of 1596. On October 8, 1594, the States-General of Holland granted him a formal licence to publish, but the book was not then ready, although parts of it seem to have been informally circulated, and all its chief suggestions were known to and discussed among the leaders of Dutch commerce during 1595.

In compiling his great book Linschoten was greatly helped by the eminent scholar, Bernard ten Broecke, the physician of Enkhuizen, who in the world of letters was known as *Paludanus*, the Latin equivalent of his surname, for scholars were still ashamed to be known as John Brewer and Jim Baker. Many of the notes and not a few passages interpolated into the text are from the hand of Paludanus, whose comments, though learned enough, are not always as much in touch with fact and nature as could be desired.

The *Itinerario* is divided into three principal books or parts, the first containing the narrative of the journey proper, in ninety-nine chapters, running to six hundred and twenty-seven pages in the Hakluyt Society's (1885) reprint of the English translation of 1598. In the second part (the first to be published, in 1595) is a collection of the routes from Europe to East and West Indies alike, in many cases translated from unpublished manuscripts of Portuguese and Spanish pilots; here is also an abundant mass of notes on the routes of the China seas. This part of Linschoten's work had great political importance; it served as the chief guide to the Dutch fleets in their early expeditions to the East, and in their first attempts to wrest the mastery of the Indies from Spain and Portugal. In the third part we have a brief description of the East and West coasts of Africa and a fuller account of America, mostly taken from earlier writers, such as Lopez on the Congo; Jean de Lery on Brazil; Peter Martyr and Oviedo on America in general. The *Itinerario* was originally illustrated by thirty-six maps, plans, and copperplate illustrations; in the Old English version of 1598 there are twenty-one topographical plates and thirty-two portraits and views. The world-map in the Dutch edition professes to be by J. Bapt. Vrient of Antwerp, famous as the publisher who bought the *Atlas* of Ortelius, and brought out an enlarged edition of the same. In the English edition the *mappe-monde* has the title *Orbis terrarum typus de integro multis in locis emendatus, Auctore Petro Plancio*, 1594; and in the left-hand corner, below the figure called *Mexicana*, is the inscription *Ioannes a Duetecum* [i.e. Doetechum] *junior fecit.* The other maps, in the English edition, include one of South-east Africa and part of the Indian Ocean, one of Western and Southern Asia from Egypt to Aracan (*imprinted at London by John Wolfe, graven by Robert Beckit*), one of Indo-China and the East Indian Archipelago, one of South Africa (*graven by William Rogers*), one of all Africa except the western hump, one of South America, one of South-western Africa and the Atlantic, one of Madagascar or St. Lawrence Island, one of Sumatra, one of Java Major, one of the Congo region, four of St. Helena (an engraved map and three profiles), one of Goa by Linschoten himself, one of Angra in Terceira (Azores), one of the two hemispheres (in small scale), and one of Spain.[1] From the resolutions of the States-General of Holland it appears that in 1592 Cornelius

[1] See De Jonge, *De opkomst van het Nederl. gezag in O. India,* vol. i. pp. 167-9; Tiele, intro. to Hak. Soc. ed. of Linschoten, pp. xvii-xix, xxx-xxxiii.

Claesz of Amsterdam, the printer and publisher of the *Itinerario*, aided by Peter Plancius, obtained a collection of sea-charts and routiers from Bartolommeo de Lasso, cosmographer to the King of Spain. The States gave Claesz a patent for printing and publishing not only the aforesaid, but also a *mappe-monde* or *land and sea-chart of the world*, drawn by Plancius and engraved by Joannes a Doetechum, as well as a chart of Asia made by an expert in the art of navigation at Goa in East India. The world-map of the *Itinerario* appears to be a reduced copy of the above-mentioned *mappe-monde* of Plancius; and extensive loans from De Lasso's collection are apparent in several of the sea-charts in Linschoten's work.

After his return from the East, Linschoten took part in the Dutch Arctic voyages of 1594 and 1595. In 1595 the first Dutch fleet sailed for the 'Indies of the Orient,' and we know from the journals of the expedition that the *Itinerario* was of the utmost value as a guide and directory. The second part of the same, comprising the Nautical Directory and Routes for the Indian and China seas, was already published (as we have pointed out) in 1595, and was greatly used on board the ships of this fleet; much also of the most important matter in the first part had been orally communicated to the leaders of the venture; and it is clear that the course of the voyage beyond the Cape of Good Hope and its special direction upon Java was due to the suggestions of Linschoten, who promised his countrymen a practical monopoly of the Java trade, 'for that the Portingales come not thither.'

In 1598 Linschoten (now settled in Enkhuizen for good) published a Dutch version of the great treatise of the Jesuit Acosta on Spanish America (*Historia natural y moral de las*

Indias), a work which he praises as far superior to the American sections of the third part of his own *Itinerario*; and in the same year Lucas Jansz Waghenaer in the preface to his new *Enkhuizen Zeekaertboek* thanks Linschoten for his help in the same, based on material derived from his northern voyages. In 1610 our traveller petitioned the States-General—unsuccessfully—for a pension; he did not long survive this rebuff; on the 8th February 1611 he died, at the very early age of forty-eight.

The *Itinerario* is one of the most valuable travel-records ever published, not only for its own subject-matter, but because it revealed to Holland and to other rivals of Spain and Portugal how weak the Eastern Empire of Philip II. really was. It thus played a most important part in exciting these rivals to active hostility in the East Indies, to the vigorous and persistent carrying out of what Drake had threatened in 1579, and Cavendish in 1587. As its political importance was speedily recognised, it soon met with readers out of the Netherlands. The famous old English translation (as well as a German) was published in 1598; two Latin versions appeared in 1599, and a French translation in 1610.

The English edition, here in part reprinted, is anonymous, but in the title to the second part (*The true and perfect description of . . . Guinea . . .*) W. P. (William Phillip?) is styled the translator. The version here given is loose, periphrastic, and super-abundant, constantly introducing words which are not in the original, and are not always warranted by the original. It also misses not infrequently the exact meaning of technical terms. On the whole, nevertheless, it gives a good broad view of all that Linschoten has to say, though it requires checking in details.

The notes of Paladanus, both in and out of the text, are omitted in the present reprint, which also abridges the text in many places,[1] and omits practically the whole of Linschoten's lengthy description of Indian lands, manners, markets, products, peoples, fauna and flora, extending from chapter v. to chapter xcii., from vol. i. p. 43 to vol. ii. p. 158 in the Hakluyt Society's edition of the complete Old English translation (1596-1885; see pp. 1-126 of this volume).[2]

Passing by the next two tracts, both relating to the destruction of Spanish and Portuguese Carracks in 1592-4 by English seamen (see vol. ii. pp. 129-150), we come to the *Miserable Captivity of Richard Hasleton* (pp. 151-180), originally printed in 1595, under the title *Strange and Wonderful Things happened to Rd. Hasleton, born at Braintree in Essex, in his ten years' travels in many foreign countries.* This is illustrated by various cuts, said to be taken from Poliphilo. The scene on p. 157, where Hasleton, urged to take the cross into his hand, spits in the inquisitor's face, is very typical; not less so is the protest on p. 168, 'Can any man which understandeth the absurd blindness and wilful ignorance of the Spanish tyrants, or Romish monsters, think them to be of the true Church? which defend their faith with fire, sword, and hellish torments.' . . . In

[1] *E.g.* pp. 3, 14, 15, 16, 17, 18, 19, 21, vol. ii. of the present collection.

[2] Much has been written, and more conjectured, about early Portuguese knowledge of the interior of Africa, the great lakes, the Nile sources, etc. A valuable hint as to this is afforded by a passage in Linschoten, Hak. Soc. edn., i. 31; this is omitted in our present reprint, but properly occurs after the words *mine named Monomotapa* on p. 17 of vol. ii.: 'in the which land is a great lake out of which you may perceive the river Nilus to spring forth, as likewise the great and wide river of Cuama or Niger [Quilimane? *i.e.* Zambesi], which runneth between Sofala and Mozambique into the sea. This, taken in connection with the Pigafetta map of 1591, may well be thought to prove a remarkable though unsifted and often vague knowledge of Upland Africa among the sixteenth century Portuguese.

Hasleton, even better than in Phillips or Hartop, we have the perfect prototype of Salvation Yeo.

Hakluyt's note (pp. 182-5) on the antiquity of English trade in the Levant, which follows, traces this East Mediterranean commerce or 'Turkey Trade,' grown to such importance under Elizabeth, from the early years of Henry VIII. (1511, 1512, etc.); while the voyage of the Earl of Cumberland, in 1589, to the Azores (pp. 186-212) forms an interesting chapter in the English counter-stroke after the ruin of the Spanish Armada of 1588; just as the fight of the *Dolphin* against five Turkish men-of-war, off Cagliari in Sardinia, in 1616, is a typical episode in the constant struggle of Mediterranean trade against Moslem piracy (see vol. ii. pp. 213-220). The Battle of Lepanto had scotched but not killed the snake: Europe was not finally freed from Mohammedan pirates until the French conquest of Algiers in 1830, though during the seventeenth century the nuisance was reduced to small dimensions.

Edward Wright, the annalist of Lord Cumberland's 1589 voyage, was the greatest scientific geographer of Elizabethan England. He was born about 1558, at Garveston in Norfolk, and became a Fellow of Caius, Cambridge, in 1587, soon after which he devoted himself to the study of navigation as a branch of mathematics. His most famous work, *Certain Errors in Navigation*, was published in 1599, and in 1614 he was appointed Lecturer in Navigation to the East India Company. He died in 1615, having won the position of the 'English Mercator' by his emended form of the famous projection of Gerard Kaufmann ('Mercator'), originally published in 1556. The present narrative is extracted from *Certain Errors in Navigation* (cf. also Purchas's *Pilgrimes*, iv. 1142-4, ed. of 1625).

Sir Francis Drake revived (see vol. ii. pp. 221-294) is an account of the so-called 'third' West Indian voyage of the great leader, that of 1572-3 to the Spanish Main. The region of Tierra Firme, or Golden Castille, then formed part, officially, of the Province of Hispaniola (Española), whose capital was at San Domingo. Since the discovery of the Peruvian silver mines in 1545, its ports had acquired immense importance as the points from which most of the treasure was shipped to Europe. We have already met with Drake in connection with the Hawkins voyages; it may be well to add here that he was born at Crowndale, near Tavistock, in Devonshire, in or about 1545; and made his first voyage to the West Indies with Captain Lovell in 1565-6, his second American voyage with Hawkins in the disastrous venture of 1567-8, his third (so far as known) in 1570, his fourth in 1571. The expedition of 1572-3 was in reality, therefore, his fifth to the New World. All the three latter claimed to be (as we are told in *Drake revived*; see vol. ii. p. 228) voyages of revenge, attempts to pay back to Spain the personal injuries received at Rio de la Hacha in his first venture, and at San Juan de Ulua ('Ulloa') in his second. They were also probably intended as diversions in the larger political struggle of England and Elizabeth against the Counter-Reformation, which assumed so acute a form in 1569-70.

As pirates, filibusters, and leviers of private war in the West Indies, Drake and the other English raiders of this time were preceded by French Huguenots, who sacked Havana as far back as 1536, and since that time had made incessant attacks upon the Spanish-American settlements of the Atlantic seaboard, until their success emboldened them to attempt a permanent colonisation within the Spanish sphere of interest in Florida (1565).[1]

The only account of Drake's raid of 1570 is in a paper of Spanish origin (*A Summary Relation of the Robberies done by Fr. Drake*), which describes it as accomplished by a vessel of only forty tons, captained by Drake ('with whom there went a merchant of Exeter called Rich. Dennys'). The same authority declares 'upon the coast of Nombre de Dios they did rob divers barks in the river Chagres that were transporting merchandise of 40,000 ducats of velvets and taffetas, . . . besides gold and silver in other barks.'

The voyage of 1571 was almost equally 'rich and gainful,' and it was now that Drake discovered his 'Port Pheasant,' probably the 'Puerto Escondido' or 'Hidden Haven' of the Spaniards, about four leagues south-west of the modern 'Caledonian Bay,' in the Gulf of Darien (see vol. ii. p. 229, etc.). The capacities of this as a base for future attacks upon the Spanish Main he saw at once, and in *Drake revived* the extreme importance of the position is apparent throughout. According to Lope de Vega,[2] the English captain (supposed to speak excellent Spanish) had visited Nombre de Dios disguised as a Spaniard; and his accurate knowledge of the topography in 1572 may be taken as some proof of the story of the *Dragontea*. Now also Drake gained a thorough knowledge of the treasure route from Peru to Panama, and across the isthmus to Nombre de Dios, where ships bound for Spain waited for their cargo.

To seize these treasures was clearly lawful for a true

[1] Just as in the same generation they attempted under Coligny's inspiration to plant themselves within the Portuguese sphere in Brazil (1558).

[2] *Dragontea*, canto i. On the other hand, it is disputed whether Drake as yet spoke Spanish at all.

Protestant hater of Spain, whether his country were or were not in a state of formal war with Philip II. Drake had it from the chaplain of his own ship that he might justly recover his losses (of 1566 and 1568) from those who had injured him; in fact, the 'case was clear in sea divinity, and few are such infidels as not to believe doctrines which make for their profit.'[1]

The spring of 1572, in which began the voyage whose story we have in *Drake revived*,[2] saw the start of a number of French and English vessels, half-traders, half-privateers, for Spanish America,—some twenty from Havre, at least two (besides Drake himself) from England. One of these was under James Ranse or Raunce,[3] probably the former master of the *William and John* in Hawkins' last voyage; the other was captained by John Garrett, probably the master of the *Minion* which escaped with such difficulty from the San Juan de Ulua fight in the venture of 1567-8. Raunce joined Drake off the Spanish Main a little later in this same year (see vol. ii. pp. 232-3); Garrett left

[1] Fuller, *Holy State*, p. 124 (ed. of 1648).

[2] Froude (*English Seamen*, pp. 108-9; ed. of 1895) is the only person who has challenged the authenticity of *Sir Francis Drake revived*, without any adequate reasons given or apparently forthcoming. The value of this booklet is of the first order; from it we derive almost all our knowledge of Drake's early feats in the West Indies and Spanish Main. From the dedication to Elizabeth, dated January 1, 1592-3, and written by Sir Francis himself, it would look as if, according to Court custom, he had presented the manuscript to the queen as a New Year's gift (cf. Corbett, *Drake*, i. 422).

Spanish versions of this expedition, strikingly confirmatory of *Drake revived*, may be found in the Record Office Manuscript 'Spanish State Papers,' xviii., of January 1580, called *Memoria de los Cossarios Ingleses que han hecho robas en las Indias*. In this paper the names of various owners of shipping captured or destroyed by Drake are given, along with a fairly minute account of the other English depredations. We may also cf. Hakluyt's extract from the *Discourse of Lopez Vaz, a Portugal*, and Duro, *Armada española*, ii. 506.

[3] Also spelt Rause or Rouse.

a warning for him at Port Pheasant that his hiding-place had been discovered (see vol. ii. p. 230).

All these ventures—Drake's, Raunce's, and Garrett's—appear to have had powerful backing: one authority[1] makes Drake the partner of Wynter and Hawkins. It is clear that behind him was a powerful group of navy men, merchants, and even statesmen, and that his little squadron was admirably fitted out, not for the execution of an irregular and independent freebooting scheme, but rather for one that needed the best equipment that England could give.

The 'Cimaroons,' Drake's native allies, who play so large a part in the narrative, were descendants of escaped negroes and 'Indian' women whom the Spaniards called 'Cimarones' or 'Hill-folk,' and the English sailors 'Maroons,' a name of pleasantly confused idea.

It has well been pointed out[2] that the nature and proportion of the arms served out to the landing party which attacked, took, but failed to hold Nombre de Dios, prove 'the action not of a mere pirate arming his desperadoes to the teeth, but of a man acquainted with the arrangement of a regular infantry *tertia*.' The absence of defensive armour was a concession to the incurable prejudice of English seamen in this matter, so much lamented by Sir Richard Hawkins,[3] so stoutly defended by others.

The great scene in the narrative (vol. ii. p. 269), where Drake gains his first view of the Pacific and prays for 'life

[1] The Ashmole Manuscripts referred to by Corbett, *Drake*, i. 159. On the other hand, Hawkins evidently felt bitterly about Drake's desertion of him after the disaster of 1568 (see note, p. 62).

[2] Cf. Corbett, *Drake*, i. 164-5.

[3] Cf. Rich. Hawkins's *Observations* (Hak. Soc. Ed.), pp. 302-4 (esp. 303-4), 'All men of good understanding, he declares, will condemn such desperate ignorance.'

and leave to sail once in an English ship in that sea,' has been justly seized upon by all who have studied Elizabethan history with any intelligence. It is indeed a decisive moment in the history of the English people as well as in the story of Drake's life: 'from that time forward his mind was pricked on continually night and day to perform his vow.'[1]

The French captain, Têtu of 'Newhaven' or Havre, who joined the English raiders on March 23, 1573 (see vol. ii. pp. 283-4, etc.), was perhaps the pilot Guillaume Le Testu of Françoise de Grâce, who published an atlas in 1555 which he dedicated to Coligny; the scimitar he gave Drake was a present from the Admiral of France, and (as our narrative says on p. 284) formerly belonged to 'Monsieur Strozze,' otherwise the Condottiere Strozzi.'[2]

Lastly, we may notice that the incident of the re-discovery and recovery of the buried treasure by the Spaniards (as mentioned in the narrative, vol. ii. p. 290) is confirmed in the *Dragontea* of Lope de Vega; just as the statement about the prizes taken (vol. ii. pp. 293-4) is borne out in general terms by the Spanish official complaint, which names several of Drake's captures, and adds that he took many other frigates engaged in the coasting trade of Tierra Firme and Veragua, with a great quantity of gold, silver, and merchandise. Among these prizes were a number of frigates newly built, at Havana and elsewhere, by the energy and skill of Pero Menendez de Aviles. For this terrible enemy of the Florida Huguenots was not merely a butcher of 'Lutherans' ('I do this not as to Frenchmen but as to heretics'), he was also the man who gradually equipped the Spanish Indies with some kind of defensive system, and to whom Philip II. owed the wisest

[1] Camden. [2] See Corbett, *Drake*, i. 190; Margry, *Navigations françaises*, 138-9.

advice he ever received from a subject in naval matters. It was with two of these new frigates that Drake and his company came home, and their merit is strikingly shown by the speed of the return voyage, which was accomplished in twenty-three days, from Cape San Antonio in Florida to the Scilly Isles (see vol. ii. pp. 293-4). Of the two vessels with which the 'Dragon' sailed from Plymouth, the *Pasha* was apparently abandoned at the close of the campaign: the scuttling of the original *Swan* is described on pp. 244-6.

Robert Knox's *Captivity in the Highlands of Ceylon* (1660-79), the last item in the present collection, is also the longest and one of the most interesting (see vol. ii. pp. 295-429). In the original edition of 1681 it has the title of *An Historical Relation of the Island of Ceylon in the East Indies, together with an Account of the detaining in captivity* [of] *the author*, etc.; there is a preface by Robert Hooke, M.D., who probably helped Knox to some extent in the polishing of his work. It is the earliest detailed account of Ceylon in English,[1] and by far the most valuable study of the interior which had been made in any European language up to this time. A Dutch translation appeared in 1692, a French one in 1693, a German in 1747. Robert Knox was born in 1640 or 1641, and lived till 1720. His father, a Scotsman of strong Puritan principles, had the same name as himself, and was, as we see from the narrative, a commander in the East India Company's service. He was made prisoner with his son and died on Feb. 9, 1660, leaving his unfortunate boy to grow to middle age in captivity. The latter, miserable as he usually was, employed his time admirably in observing and recording native customs, natural features, and recent Cinghalese

[1] Cf. vol. i. of Harris' *Navigantium Bibliotheca*, pp. 678, 811, 844, 938.

tradition After his escape he seems to have developed a morose temper and decided roughness of manner: his hatred of women was vehemently expressed in his letters: in Ceylon he rejects all offers of alliance with native females simply from the fear of thus increasing the difficulty of his escape.

Knox's captivity occurred during the long reign of Raja Singha II. (1635-85), the one hundred and seventy-second king since Vijaya, in B.C. 543, came from Palibothra on the Ganges to the sacred isle of *Lanka*.

'Ceylon was well known to the ancients under the name of Taprobane,' so every manual will tell us; but unquestionably under that name there is often a confusion between our Sumatra and Ceylon itself: both in Ptolemy (as 'Taprobane'), and in the *Periplus of the Erythraean Sea* (as 'Palaesimundus'), it appears as an island of gigantic size. Onesicritus and Megasthenes, Strabo and Pliny, all have something to say of Taprobane; under Claudius, Julian, Theodosius II., and Justinian, intercourse with the Roman Empire is recorded; and the names of Annius Plocamus in the first century, of Scholasticus in the fifth, of Sopater and Cosmas Indicopleustes in the sixth, have been preserved as those of visitors from the Mediterranean world to *Sielediva*. In the same way Fa Hien (*c.* A.D. 410) and Khi-nie (*c.* 970) made their way thither from the opposite end of the 'Habitable World'—from that 'Land of Han,' 'Celestial,' or 'Middle' Kingdom which had so close a bond with all centres of Buddhist faith, literature, and relic-treasure.

[1] In Ptolemy (*c.* A.D. 130) it is drawn as larger than Spain, and occupying most of the space that should have been given to the Indian Peninsula; in the *Periplus*, *c.* A.D. 90, it is described as of immense length, roughly like the shape of our Sumatra, but far greater, and bearing no perceptible resemblance to Ceylon.

Hiouen-Thsang (A.D. 628-649), however, the greatest of Chinese travellers, though he evidently longed to see the matchless jewels of Ceylon, did not touch there himself.

In the first half of the fifteenth century (1405-59), the island appears to have paid tribute to China, renewing then in more tangible form a shadowy allegiance of the earlier Middle Ages.

Among the Christian travellers [1] of the Mediæval Period who reached Southern and Eastern Asia, many refer to Ceylon, but few visited it, before the discovery of the ocean route round the Cape. Marco Polo and Bishop John de Marignolli are exceptions (*c.* A.D. 1293-4, and 1347-9). Even Nicolo Conti, though perhaps the first European to describe the cinnamon of *Seyllan*, does not seem to have landed (*c.* 1440).

On the other hand, the Arabs were constant visitors. Fa Hien found them there, two centuries before Mohammed. *Serendib* is one of the best-known points in the ninth and tenth century geography of Suleyman the merchant, Abu Zeyd Hassan, and Sindbad the Sailor; one of the clearest accounts of Ceylon before the advent of the Portuguese is that of the 'Doctor of Tangier,' Ibn Batuta (*c.* 1336 A.D.).

After Diego Cão, Bartholomew Diaz, Covilhão, and Vasco da Gama had opened the African or S.E. route to the Indies, an Italian trader, Girolamo di S. Stefano of Genoa, stayed a very short time in the island in 1498 or 1499. In 1506, the great traveller Ludovico di Varthema of Bologna, journeying by 'Arab' routes, touched at a port on the

[1] Friar Odoric of Pordenone, Bishop Jordanus of Columbum (Quilon), and John of Hesse are among the 'Latins' who wrote most fully of Seyllan or Sillan, but did not make a personal inspection.

west coast: as usual, he contrives to give more information in ten lines than most men in ten chapters.

The Portuguese knew Ceylon, as a coveted possession, from 1505, when under their boy-leader Lawrence or Lourenço, the hero son of the first Viceroy, Francisco de Almeyda, they attempted to gain a footing in the island, at Point de Galle. Affonso de Albuquerque (1509-15), as second Governor-General, seems to have meant to establish a fortress on some point of the coast; but the actual Portuguese dominion only began in 1517, when Lopo Soares de Albergaria appeared before Colombo and obtained permission to build a 'castle' there. The natives soon repented of their concession, and attacked the new settlement in force. Being vigorously repulsed, they acknowledged themselves, according to the conquerors' version, tributaries and vassals of the King of Portugal (see Camoens, *Lusiads*, x. 51). It is clear, however, that the people of the hilly upland struggled pretty successfully against the permanent extension of the Portuguese dominion. In 1542, and again in 1581, the dying rulers of 'Condé,' or Kandy, bequeathed their dominions to the Europeans, and in 1547-50 the Portuguese almost established themselves in the central fastnesses. In 1593-5 they did actually gain momentary possession of Kandy; and in 1560 they carried off and burnt the original tooth-relic of Buddha; but all these successes were transient. The Cinghalese refused to be willed away to foreign masters, and succeeded in repulsing each advance of their enemy, beyond the coastal lowlands. At the end of the sixteenth century, Linschoten (though perhaps with exaggeration) describes Colombo as the only real possession of the subjects of Philip II. in the island, 'which by mere force and great charges is maintained, for that they have no other place or piece of ground, no not one foot but that in all the land.' (See Linschoten, *Itinerario*, book i. chaps. xiii., xiv., xcii.). In 1587-8, Raja Singha I. fiercely but unsuccessfully attacked this 'small, strong, well-guarded' fort; and in 1595 the extreme barbarities of the would-be conqueror, Jerome de Azavedo, failed to crush the resistance of a people whom he drove to despair. Though he occupied Kandy, he could not make his raid produce any lasting results.

The Dutch paid their first visit to Ceylon in 1602; and between 1638 and 1658 they wholly expelled the Portuguese, substituting themselves as masters at Trincomali in 1639, at Point de Galle in 1640, at Colombo in 1656. Their timid and irresolute policy towards the native powers (as well as the studied cruelty of the Portuguese) is well brought out in Knox's narrative (see esp. ii. pp. 409-420). Here also is a very early notice of that vigorous onward movement of the French, which, in 1672, brought them from Madagascar, Bourbon, and the Isle de France to Ceylon and the Coromandel Coast, and which in spite of all discouragements continued apparently to prosper and progress till Dupleix made France for a moment (1742-50) the dominant power in the Deccan (see vol. ii. pp. 421-25).

The Cinghalese practice of detaining white visitors was not at all peculiar. Instances of it are common enough among semi-civilised nations: the most famous example, perhaps, is that of Abyssinia, where, to give only one instance among many, the first Portuguese envoy to the court of Prester John, Pero de Covilhão, was kept as a hostage to the day of his death (from 1490 to 1520).

C. RAYMOND BEAZLEY.

Oct. 24th, 1902.

To the Right Worshipful Sir WILLIAM THOMSON Knight, Governor; THOMAS PAPILLON Esquire, Deputy; and the 24 "Committees" of the Honourable East India Company hereunder specified, viz:—

The Rt. Hon. GEORGE, Earl of BERKLEY.
The Rt. Hon. JAMES, Lord CHANDOS.
Sir MATTHEW ANDREWS Knight.
Sir JOHN BANKS Baronet.
Sir SAMUEL BARNARDISTON Baronet
Mr. CHRISTOPHER BOONE.
JOHN BATHURST Esquire.
Sir JOSIAH CHILD Baronet.
Mr. THOMAS CANHAM.
Colonel JOHN CLERK.
Sir JAMES EDWARDS Knight.
Mr. JOSEPH HERNE.
RICHARD HUTCHINSON Esquire.
JAMES HUBLON Esquire.
Sir JOHN LETHIEULLIER Knight.
Mr. NATHANIEL PETTON.
Sir JOHN MOOR Knight.
SAMUEL MOYER Esquire.
Mr. JOHN MORDEN.
Mr. JOHN PAIGE.
EDWARD RUDGE Esquire.
DANIEL SHELDON Esquire.
Mr. JEREMY SAMBROOK.
ROBERT THOMSON Esquire.

RIGHT WORSHIPFUL,

SINCE my return home to my native country of England, after a long and disconsolate captivity; my friends and acquaintance, in our converse together, have been inquisitive into the state of that land in which I was captivated: whose curiosity I endeavoured to satisfy. But my relations and accounts of things in those parts were so strange and uncouth, and so different from those in the Western nations; and withal, my discourses seeming so delightful and acceptable unto them: they very frequently called upon me to write what I knew of that island of Ceylon, and to digest it into a discourse, and make it more public. Unto which motion, I was not much unwilling; partly that I might comply with the desires and counsels of my friends; and chiefly, that I might publish and declare the great mercy of GOD to me, and commemorate, before all men, my singular deliverance out of that strange and pagan land: which—as often as I think of, or mention—I cannot but admire, and adore the goodness of GOD towards me; there being in it, so many notable footsteps of His signal providence.

I had then by me several papers, which—during my voyage homewards from Bantam, at leisure times—I wrote concerning the King and the country; and concerning the English there; and of my escape: which papers I forthwith set myself to peruse and draw into a method; and to add what more might occur to my thoughts of these matters. Which, at length, I have finished; contriving what I had to relate, under four heads. The first, concerning the country, and products of it. The second, concerning the King and his government. The third, concerning the inhabitants, and their religion and customs. And the last, concerning our surprise, detainment, and escape. In all which, I take leave to declare that I have written nothing but either what I am assured of by my own personal knowledge to be true, and wherein I have borne a great, and a sad share: or what I have received from the inhabitants themselves, of such things as are commonly known to be true among them.

The book being thus perfected; it required no long meditation unto whom to present it. It could be to none but yourselves, my honoured Masters, by whose wisdom and success the East Indian parts of the world are now nearly as well known as the countries next adjacent to us. So that by your means, not only the wealth, but the knowledge of those Indies is brought home to us.

Unto your favour and patronage, therefore, Right Worshipful, I humbly presume to recommend these papers and the author of them; who rejoiceth at this opportunity to acknowledge the favours you have already conferred on him; and to profess that—next unto GOD—on you depend his future hopes and expectations. Being

Right Worshipful,

Your most obliged, and most humble and devoted servant to be commanded,

ROBERT KNOX.

London.
18*th March* 1681.

To the Right Worshipful the Governor, the Deputy Governor, and Four and Twenty "Committees" of the Honourable the East India Company, viz:

Sir JOSIAH CHILD Baronet, Governor.
THOMAS PAPILION Esquire, Deputy.

The Rt. Hon. GEORGE, Earl of BERKLEY.
Sir JOSEPH ASHE Baronet.
Sir SAMUEL BARNARDISTON Baronet.
Mr. CHRISTOPHER BOONE.
Mr. THOMAS CANHAM.
Colonel JOHN CLERKE.
Mr. JOHN CUDWORTH.
JOHN DUBOIS Esquire.
Sir JAMES EDWARDS Knight and Alderman.
RICHARD HUTCHINSON Esquire.

Mr. JOSEPH HERNE.
Mr. WILLIAM HEDGES.
Sir JOHN LAWRENCE Knight and Alderman.
Mr. NATHANIEL LETTON.
Sir JOHN MOORE Knight and Alderman.
SAMUEL MOYER Esquire.
Mr. JOHN MORDEN.
Mr. JOHN PAIGE.
EDWARD RUDGE Esquire.
Mr. JEREMY SAMBROOKE.
Mr. WILLIAM SEDGWICK.
ROBERT THOMSON Esquire.
SAMUEL THOMSON Esquire.
JAMES WARD Esquire.

RIGHT WORSHIPFUL,

WHAT I formerly presented you in writing, having in pursuance of your commands now somewhat dressed by the help of the Graver and the Printer; I a second time humbly tender to you. 'Tis, I confess, at best too mean a return for your great kindness to me. Yet I hope you will not deny it a favourable acceptance; since it is the whole return I made from the Indies after twenty years' stay there: having brought home nothing else but

(who is also wholly at your service and command)

ROBERT KNOX.

London,
1st of *August* 1681.

NINETEEN YEARS' CAPTIVITY

IN THE KINGDOM OF CONDE UDA.

BY

Captain ROBERT KNOX.

PRELIMINARY CHAPTER I.

A general description of the Island.

HOW THIS island lies with respect unto the neighbouring coasts, I shall not speak at all, that being to be seen in our ordinary sea cards [*charts*] which describe those parts); and but little concerning the maritime parts of it, now under the jurisdiction of the Dutch: my design being to relate such things only that are new and unknown unto these European nations. It is the inland country therefore I chiefly intend to write of: which is yet a hidden land; even to the Dutch themselves that inhabit upon the island. For I have seen among them a fair large map of this place; the best I believe extant, yet very faulty. The ordinary maps in use among us are much more so. I have procured a new one to be drawn with as much truth and exactness as I could: and his judgment will not be deemed altogether inconsiderable, who had for twenty years travelled about the island, and knew almost every step of those parts: especially those that most want describing.

I begin with the sea coasts: of all which the Hollander is master. On the north end; the chief places are Jaffnapatam and the island of Manaar. On the east side, Trincomalee and Batticalloe. To the south, is the city of Point de Galle. On the west, the city of Colombo; so called from a tree, the natives call *ambo* (which bears the mango fruit) growing in that place, which never bare fruit but only leaves, which in their language is *cola*; and hence they called the tree *Colambo*: which the Christians, in honour of COLUMBUS, turned to Colombo. It is the chief city on the sea coasts, where the Dutch Governor hath his residence. On this west side also are Negombo and Calpentyn. All these already mentioned are strong fortified places. There are besides many other smaller forts and fortifications: all which, with considerable territories; to wit, all round bordering upon the sea coasts, belong to the Dutch nation.

I proceed to the inland country, being that that is now under the King of Kandy. It is convenient that we first understand that this land is divided into greater or lesser shares or parts. The greater divisions give me leave to call Provinces, and the lesser, Counties; as resembling ours in England, though not altogether so big.

On the north parts, lie the Province of Nuwerakalawe, consisting of five lesser divisions or counties: the Province also of Hotkorle, signifying "Seven Counties;" it contains seven counties.

On the eastward, is Matella, containing three counties. There are also lying on that side Tammaukadua, Bintenne, Vellas, Panowa. These are single counties. Oowah also, containing three counties: in this province are two and thirty of the King's captains dwelling, with their soldiers.

In the mid-land, within those already mentioned, lie Wallaponahoy, it signifies "Fifty holes or vales," which describe the nature of it, being nothing but hills and valleys —Poncipot, signifying "Five hundred soldiers"—Goddaponahoy, signifying "Fifty pieces of dry land"—Hevoihattay, signifying "Sixty soldiers"—Kottemalle—Horsepot [? *Harasia Pattoo*], "Four hundred soldiers"—Tunponahoy [? *Tumpane*], "Three fifties"—Oodanowera, it signifies "The Upper City;" where I lived last, and had land—Yattenowera, "The Lower City," in which stands the royal and chief city Kandy.

These two counties I last named, have the pre-eminence of all the rest in the land. They are most populous and fruitful. The inhabitants thereof are the chief and principal men: insomuch that it is a usual saying among them, that "if they want a king, they may take any man of either of these two counties from the plough, and wash the dirt off him; and he—by reason of his quality and descent—is fit to be a king." And they have this peculiar privilege; that none may be their Governor, but one born in their own country.

These that follow, lie to the westward. Ooddaboolat—Dollosbage—Hotterakorle, containing four counties—Portaloon—Tunkorle, containing three counties—Kottiaar. Which last, together with Batticalloe and a part of Tunkorle; the Hollander took from the king, during my being there.

There are about ten or twelve more unnamed; next bordering on the coast; which are under the Hollander.

All these Provinces and Counties, excepting six—Tammankadua, Vellas, Panowa, Hotterakorle, Hotkorle, and Nuwerakalawe—lie upon hills, fruitful and well watered: and therefore are they called in one word, Conde Uda; which signifies, "On top of the hills;" and the king is styled, the King of Conde Uda.

All these counties are divided, each from other, by great woods; which none may fell, being preserved for fortifications. In most of them are Watches kept constantly; but in troublesome times, in all.

The land is full of hills, but exceedingly well watered; there being many pure and clear rivers running through them: which falling down about their lands is a very great benefit for the country; in respect to their rice, their chief substance. These rivers are generally very rocky, and so unnavigable. In them are great quantities of fish; and the greater, for want of skill in the people to catch them.

The main river of all is called Mahavilla Ganga; which proceeds out of the mountain called Adam's Peak (of which afterwards). It runs through the whole land northward, and falls into the sea at Trincomalee. It may be an arrow's flight over in breadth; but not navigable, by reason of the many rocks and great falls in it. Towards the sea, it is full of alligators; but among the mountains there are none at all. It is so deep that, except it be mighty dry weather, a man cannot wade over it; unless towards the head of it. They use little canoes to pass over it: but there are no bridges built over it, it being so broad, and the stream in the time of rains—which in this country are very great—runs so high; that they cannot make them; neither if they could, would it be permitted. For the King careth not to make his country easy to travel in; but desires to keep it intricate. This river runs within a mile or less of the city of Kandy. In some places of it, it is full of rocks; in others, clear for three or four miles.

There is another large river [*Kottemalle Oya*] running through Kottemalle; and falls into that before mentioned. There are divers other brave rivers that water the country; though none navigable, for the cause above said.

The land is generally covered with woods; excepting the kingdom of Oowah, and the counties of Ooddaboolat and Dollosbage, which are, naturally, somewhat clear of them.

It is most populous about the middle; least near about by the sea. How it is with those parts under the Hollander, I know not. The northern parts are somewhat sickly by reason of bad water. The rest are very healthful.

The valleys between their hills are, many of them, quagmires: and most of them full of brave springs of pure water: which watery valleys are the best sort of land for their corn, as requiring much moisture.

On the south side of Conde Uda is a hill, supposed to be highest on the island, called in the Cingalese language Hamalell; but by the Portuguese and the European nations, Adam's Peak. It is sharp like a sugar loaf; and has on the top a flat stone with the print of a foot, like a man's but far bigger, being about two feet long. The people of the land count it meritorious to go and worship this impression: and generally about their new year, which is in March; they—men, women, and children—go up this vast and high mountain to worship.

Out of this mountain arise many fine rivers, which run through the land; some to the westward, some to the southward, and the main river—the Mahavilla Ganga before mentioned—to the northward.

This kingdom of Conde Uda is strongly fortified by nature. For which way soever you enter into it; you must ascend vast and high mountains, and descend little or nothing. The ways are many; but very narrow, so that but one can go abreast. The hills are covered with woods and great rocks, so that it is scarcely possible to get up anywhere, but only in the paths. In all of which, there are Gates made of thorns—the one at the bottom, the other at the top of the hills—and two or three men always set to watch: who are tc examine all that come and go, and see what they carry; that letters may not be conveyed, nor prisoners or other slaves run away. These Watches, in case of opposition, are to call out to the towns near; who are to assist them. They oftentimes have no arms, for they are people of the next towns: but their weapons to stop people, are to charge them in the King's name; which being disobeyed, is so severely punished, that none dare resist. These Watches are but as sentinels to give notice; for in case of war and danger, the King sends commanders and soldiers to lie here.

The one part of this island differs very much from the other, both in respect of the seasons and the soil. For when the westwardly winds [*the S.-W. monsoon*] blow, then it rains on the west side of the island; and that is the season for them to till their grounds: and at the same time, on the east side is very fair and dry weather, and the time of their harvest. On the contrary, when the east winds [*the N.-E. monsoon*] blow, it is tilling time for those that inhabit the east parts, and harvest to those on the west. So harvest is there, in one part or other, all the year long. These rains and this dry weather do part themselves about the middle of the land; as oftentimes I have seen: there being on the one side of a mountain called Cauragas Hing, rainy and wet weather: and as soon as I came on the other side, dry and so exceeding hot, that I could scarcely walk on the ground; being—as the manner there is—barefooted.

It rains far more in the high lands of Conde Uda, than in the low lands beneath the hills. The north end of this island is much subject to dry weather. I have known it, for five or six years together, so dry, having no rain—and there is no other means of water but that; there being but three springs of running water there, that I know or ever heard of—that they could not plough nor sow, and scarcely could dig wells deep enough to get water to drink; and when they got it, its taste was brackish. At which time, in other parts, there wanted not rain: whither the northern people were forced to come and buy food.

Let thus much suffice to have spoken of the countries, soil, and nature of this island in general. I will proceed to speak of the cities and towns in it; together with some other remarkable matters thereunto belonging.

PRELIMINARY CHAPTER II.

Concerning the chief cities and towns of this Island.

IN THIS island are several places where, they say formerly stood cities, and which still retain the name; though little or nothing of building be now to be seen: but there are five cities now standing, which are the most eminent, and where the King hath palaces and goods; yet even these—all of them, except that wherein his person is,—are ruined and fallen to decay.

The first is the city of Kandy—so generally called by the Christians, probably from Conde, which in the Cingalese language signifies "hills," for among them it is situated—but by the inhabitants called Hingodagul-newera, as much as to say, "The City of the Cingalese people;" and Mauneur, signifying "The chief or royal city." This is the chief or metropolitical city of the whole island. It is placed in the midst of the island, in the Province of Yattenowera; bravely situated for all conveniences, excellently well watered. The King's palace stands on the east corner of the city, as is customary in this land for the King's palaces to stand. This city is three square, like a triangle, but has no artificial strength about it: unless on the south side, which is the easiest and openest way to it, where they have long since cast up a bank of earth across the valley from one hill to another; which nevertheless is not so steep but that a man may easily go over it anywhere. It may be some twenty feet in height. In every way to come to this city, about two or three miles off from it, are Thorn Gates and Watches to examine all that go and come. It is environed around with hills. The great river [*the Mahavilla Ganga*] coming down from Adam's Peak, runs within less than a mile of it, on the west side.

It has oftentimes been burnt by the Portuguese in their former invasions of this island; together with the King's palace and the temples. Insomuch that the King has been fain to pay them a tribute of three elephants *per annum*. The King left this city, about twenty years ago [i.e. *about* 1660], and never since has come to it. So that it is now quite gone to decay.

A second city is Nellembe Newera, lying in Ooddaboollat, south of Kandy, some twelve miles distant. Unto this, the King retired and here kept his Court, when he forsook Kandy.

Thirdly. The city Alloot Newera, on the north-east of Kandy. Here this King was born. Here also he keeps a great store of corn and salt, &c., against time of war or trouble. This is situated in the country of Bintenne; which land I have never been at, but have taken a view of it from the top of a mountain. It seems to be a smooth land, and not much hilly. The great river [*the Mahavilla Ganga*] runneth through the midst of it. It is all over covered with mighty woods and abundance of deer: but much subject to dry weather and sickness. In these woods are a sort of wild people [*The Veddahs, supposed to be the original race inhabiting Ceylon*] inhabiting.

Fourthly, Badoolla, eastward from Kandy, some two days' journey: the second city in this land. The Portuguese, in time of war, burnt it down to the ground. The palace here is quite ruined: the pagodas only remain in good repair.

This city stands in the kingdom or province of Oowah, which is a country well watered; the land not smooth, neither the hills very high. Wood very scarce, but what they plant about their houses: but great plenty of cattle; their land, void of wood, being the more apt for grazing. If these cattle be carried to any other parts in this island, they will commonly die. The reason whereof no man can tell. Only they conjecture it is occasioned by a kind of small tree or shrub that grows in all countries but in Oowah, the touch or scent of which may be poison to the Oowah cattle, though it is not so to other. The tree hath a pretty physical smell like an apothecary's shop; but no sort of cattle will eat it. In this country grows the best tobacco that is on the land. Rice is more in plenty here than most other things.

The fifth city is Digligy Newera, towards the east of Kandy, lying in the country of Hevahatt: where the King—ever since he was routed from Nellembe, in the rebellion, *Anno* 1664—hath held his Court. The situation of this place is very rocky and mountainous, the land is barren: so that hardly a worse place could be found out in the whole island. Yet the King chose it, partly because it lies about the middle of his kingdom, but chiefly for his safety: having the great mountain Gauluda behind his palace, unto which he fled for safety in the rebellion—being not only high, but on the top of it lie three towns, and corn fields, whence he may have necessary supplies. And it is so fenced with steep cliffs, rocks, and woods; that a few men here will be able to defend themselves against a great army.

There are, besides these already mentioned, several other ruinous places that do still retain the name of cities; where kings have reigned, though now there are little footsteps remaining of them.

At the north end of this King's dominions is one of these ruinous cities, called Anuradhapoora, where they say ninety kings have reigned; the spirits of whom they hold now to be saints in glory, having merited it by making pagodas, and stone pillars and images to the honour of their gods: whereof there are many yet remaining, which the Cingalese count very meritorious to worship, and the next way to heaven. Near by is a river by which we came, when we made our escape: all along which there is an abundance of hewn stones; some long for pillars, some broad for paving. Over this river, there have been three stone bridges, built upon stone pillars; but now are fallen down; and the country is all desolate, without inhabitants.

At this city of Anuradhapoora is a Watch kept; beyond which are no more people that yield obedience to the King of Kandy. This place is above ninety miles to the northward of the city of Kandy. In these northern parts there are no hills, nor but two or three springs of running water; so that their corn ripeneth with the help of rain.

There is a port in the country of Portaloon, on the west side of this island, whence part of the King's country is supplied with salt and fish: where they have some small trade with the Dutch; who have a fort on the point to prevent boats from coming. But the eastern parts being too far and too hilly, to drive cattle thither for salt; GOD's providence hath provided them a place on the east side, nearer to them, which in their language they called Leawava: where, the eastwardly winds blowing, the sea beats in; and in westerly winds—being then fair weather there—it becomes salt; and that in such abundance, that they have as much as they please to fetch.

This place of Leawava is so contrived by the Providence of the Almighty Creator, that neither the Portuguese nor Dutch, in all the time of their wars, could ever prevent this people from having the benefit of this salt: which is the principal thing that they esteem in time of trouble or war; and most of them do keep by them, a store of salt against such times. It is, as I have heard, environed with hills on the land side, and by sea not convenient for ships to ride: and very sickly—which they do impute to the power of a great god, who dwelleth near by in a town called Cotteragom, standing in the road; to whom all that go to fetch salt, both small and great, must give an offering. The name and power of this god striketh such terror into the Cingalese, that those who otherwise are enemies to this King, and have served both Portuguese and Dutch against him; yet, would never assist to make invasions this way.

Having said thus much concerning the cities and other eminent places of this kingdom; I will now add a little concerning their towns. The best are those that do belong to their idols, wherein stand their *Dewals* or temples. They do not care to make streets by building their houses together in rows, but each man lives by himself in his own plantation; having a hedge, it may be, and a ditch round about him to keep out cattle. Their towns are always placed some distance from the highways: for they care not that their towns should be a thoroughfare for all people; but only for those that have business with them. The towns are not very big: in some may be forty, and in some fifty houses; and in some, above an hundred: and in some again, not above eight or ten.

As I said before of their cities, so I must of their towns; that there are many of them here and there lying desolate: occasioned by their voluntarily forsaking them; which they often do, in case many of them fall sick, and two or three die soon after one another. For this, they conclude to happen from the hand of the devil; whereupon, they all leave their town, and go to another, thinking thereby to avoid him: thus relinquishing both their houses and lands too. Yet afterwards, when they think the devil hath departed the place: some will sometimes come back, and reassume their lands again.

PRELIMINARY CHAPTER III.

General character of the Cingalese, with some of their proverbs.

HERE are iron and crystal in great plenty. Saltpetre they can make. Brimstone, some say, is here; but the King will not have it discovered. Steel they can make of their iron. Ebony is in great abundance, with choice of tall and large timber. Cardamoms, jaggory, arrack, oil, black-lead, turmeric, salt, rice, betel nuts, musk, wax, pepper—which grows here very well, and might be had in great plenty, if it had any vent [*sale*]—and the peculiar commodity of the island, cinnamon. Wild cattle also, and wild honey in great plenty in the woods: it lies in holes or hollow trees, free for any that will take the pains to get it. Elephants' teeth. Cotton, of which there is good plenty, growing in their own grounds: sufficient to make them good and strong cloth for their own use, and also to sell to the people of the uplands, where cotton is not so plentiful.

All these things the land affords, and might do it in much greater quantity; if the people were but laborious and industrious. But that, they are not. For the Cingalese are naturally a people given to sloth and laziness. If they can but any ways live, they abhor to work. Only what their necessities force them to do, they do: that is, to get food and raiment.

Yet in this I must a little vindicate them. For what indeed should they do with more than food and raiment; seeing that, as their estates increase, so do their taxes also? And although the people be generally covetous, spending but little, scraping together what they can: yet such is the government they are under; that they are afraid to be known to have anything, lest it be taken away from them. Neither have they any encouragement for their industry, having no vent by traffic and commerce for what they have got.

"I have given pepper, and got ginger." Spoken when a

man makes a bad exchange: and they use it in reference to the Dutch succeeding the Portuguese in their island.

"Pick your teeth, to fill your belly." Spoken of stingy niggardly people.

"To eat before you go forth, is handsome and convenient." Which they therefore ever do.

"As the saying is, If I come to beg buttermilk, why should I hide my pan." Which is ordinarily spoken to introduce the business that one man comes to speak to another about.

"A beggar and a trader cannot be lost." Because they are never out of their way.

"To lend to another, makes him become an enemy." For he will hate you, if you ask him for it again.

"Go not with a slave in one boat." It signifies to have no dealing nor correspondence with any one's slave: for if any damage should happen, it would fall upon your head; and, by their law, you must make it good.

"First look into the hand, afterwards open the mouth." Spoken of a judge; who first must have a bribe, before he will pronounce on their side.

"Take a ploughman from the plough, and wash off his dirt: and he is fit to rule a kingdom." Spoken of the people of Conde Uda, where there are such eminent persons of the "Hondrew" rank: and because of the civility, understanding, and gravity of the poorest men among them.

"Nobody can reproach the King and the beggar." Because the former is above the slander of the people, and nothing can be said bad enough of the latter.

"Like Noya and Polonga." Denoting irreconcilable enemies.

If the Polonga and the Noya meet together, they cease not fighting till one hath killed the other.

The reason and original of this fatal enmity is this; according to a fable among the Cingalese.

These two chanced to meet in a dry season, when water was scarce. The Polonga being almost famished for thirst; asked the Noya, where he might go to find a little water. The Noya, a little before, had met with a bowl of water in which a child lay playing: as it is usual among this people, to wash their children in a bowl of water, and there leave them, to tumble and play in it. Here the Noya had quenched his thirst, but, as he was drinking, the child that lay in the bowl, out of his innocency and play, hit him on the head, with his hand; which the Noya made no matter of, but bare patiently, knowing it was not done out of any malice, and having drunk as much as sufficed him, went away, without doing the child any harm.

Being minded to direct the Polonga to this bowl, but desirous withal to preserve the child: he told him, "That he knew of water; but he was such a surly hasty creature, that he was fearful to let him know where it was, lest he might do some mischief." Making him therefore promise that he would not: he then told him, that at such a place there was a bowl of water with a child playing in it; and that probably the child might, as he was tumbling, give him a pat on the head—as he had done to him before—but charged him nevertheless, not to hurt the child. Which the Polonga having promised; went his way towards the water, as the Noya had directed him.

The Noya, knowing his touchy disposition, went after him: fearing that he might do the child a mischief; and that thereby he himself might be deprived of the like benefit afterwards. It fell out as he feared. For as the Polonga drank, the child patted him on the head: and he, in his hasty humour, bit him on the hand, and killed him. The Noya seeing this, was resolved to be revenged: and so, reproaching him for his baseness, fought him so long till he killed him; and after that, devoured him. Which to this day they ever do; and always fight, when they meet: and the conqueror eats the body of the vanquished. Hence the proverb.

"He that hath money to give to his judge, needs not fear; be his cause right or wrong." Because of the corruption of the great men, and their greediness for bribes.

"If our fortune [*gerehah*] be bad, what can god do against it?" Reckoning that none of their gods have power to reverse the fate of an ill planet.

"The ague is nothing, but the headache is all." That country is very subject to agues, which do especially afflict the heads of those who have them.

They have certain words of form and civility that they use

upon occasion. When they come to another man's house; he asks them "What they come for?" which is his civility. And they answer, "I come for nothing;" which is their ordinary reply; though they do come for something.

And upon this they have a fable. A god came down upon earth one day, and bade all his creatures come before him; and demanded, "What they would have, and it should be granted them." So all the beasts and other creatures came: and one desired strength, another legs, and another wings, &c.; and it was bestowed on them. Then came the white men. The god asked them, "What they came for?" And they said, "They desired Beauty, Valour, and Riches." It was granted them. At last, came the Cingalese. The god required of them "What they came for?" They answered, "I come for nothing." Then replied he again, "Do you come for nothing: then go away with nothing!" And so they for their compliment, fared worse than all the rest.

I might multiply many more of their proverbial sayings: but let these suffice.

The worst words they use to whites and Christians, is to call them "Beef-eating slaves."

When they travel together, a great many of them, the roads are so narrow that but one can go abreast. And if there be twenty of them, there is but one argument or matter discoursed among them all from the first to the last. And so they go talking along, all together: and every one carrieth his provisions on his back, for his whole journey.

In short. In carriage and behaviour, they are very grave and stately, like unto Portuguese; in understanding, quick and apprehensive; in design, subtle and crafty; in discourse, courteous but full of flatteries; naturally inclined to temperance both in meat and drink, but not to chastity; near and provident in their families, commending good husbandry. In their dispositions, not passionate; neither hard to be reconciled again when angry. In their promises, very unfaithful; approving lying in themselves, but misliking it in others: delighting in sloth, deferring labour till urgent necessity constrain them. Neat in apparel, nice in eating, and not given to much sleep.

PRELIMINARY CHAPTER IV.

The Thorn Gates.

THERE are constant Watches set in convenient places in all parts of the country, and Thorn Gates: but in time of danger, besides the ordinary Watches in all towns, they are in all places and at every cross road, exceedingly thick: so that it is not possible for any to pass unobserved.

These Thorn Gates which I here mention, and have done before, are made of a sort of thorn bush or thorn tree; each stick or branch whereof thrusts out on all sides round about, sharp prickles like iron nails, of three or four inches long. One of these very thorns, I have lately seen in the Repository at Gresham College. These sticks or branches being as big as a good cane, are plaited one very close to another, and so being fastened or tied to three or four upright spars, are made in the fashion of a door.

This is hung upon a door case some ten or twelve feet high (so that they may, and do ride through upon elephants) made of three pieces of timber like a gallows, after this manner ∏: the thorn door hanging upon the transverse piece like a shop window. So they lift it up or clap it down; as there is occasion: and tie it with rope to a cross bar.

But especially in all roads and passes from the city [*Digligy*] where the King now inhabits, are very strict Watches set: which will suffer none to pass, not having a passport; which is the print of a seal in clay.

It is given at the Court to them that have license to go through the Watches. The seals are different, according to the profession of the party. As to a soldier, the print of a man with a pike on his shoulder; or, to a labourer, of a man with two bags hanging at each end of a pole upon his shoulder; which is the manner they commonly carry their loads: and to a white man, the passport is the print of a man with a sword by his side and his hat on his head. And as many men as there are in the company; so many prints there must be in the clay.

There is not half the examination for those that come into the city, as for those that go out; whom they usually search to see what they carry with them.

NINETEEN YEARS' CAPTIVITY

IN THE KINGDOM OF CONDE UDA.

BY

Captain ROBERT KNOX.

CHAPTER I.

Of the reason of our going to Ceylon, and detainment there.

IN THIS fourth and last part, I purpose to speak concerning our captivity in this island; and during which, in what condition the English have lived there; and the eminent providence of GOD in my escape thence: together with other matters relating to the Dutch and other European nations that dwell, and are kept there. All which will afford so much variety and new matter, that I doubt not but the readers will be entertained with as much delight in perusing these things, as in any else that have been already related.

I begin with the unhappy occasion of our going to this country.

Anno 1657, the *Anne* frigate of London, Captain ROBERT KNOX Commander, on the 21st day of January; set sail out of the Downs in the service of the Honourable the English East India Company, bound for Fort St. George [*Madras*] on the coast of Coromandel, to trade one year from port to port in India. Which we having performed, as we were lading goods to return for England, being on the road of Malipatam, on the 19th of November, 1659, there happened such a mighty storm, that in it several ships were cast away: and we were forced to cut our mainmast by the board; which so disabled the ship that she could not proceed in her voyage. Whereupon Kottiaar in the island of Ceylon, being a very commodious bay, fit for our present distress; THOMAS CHAMBERS, Esq., since Sir THOMAS CHAMBERS, the Agent at Fort St. George, ordered that the ship should take in some cloth, and go to Kottiaar Bay [i.e. *the Bay of Trincomalee*], there to trade; while she lay, to set her mast. Where being arrived, according to the appointment of those Indian merchants of Porto Nova we carried with us, they were put ashore; and we minded our business to set another mainmast, and repair our other damages that we had sustained by the late storm.

At our first coming hither, we were shy and jealous of the people of the place; by reason our nation never had any commerce or dealing with them. But now having been there some twenty days, and going ashore and coming on board at our pleasure, without any molestation; the Governor of the place also telling us that we were welcome, as we seemed to ourselves to be: we began to lay aside all suspicious thoughts of the people dwelling thereabouts, who had very kindly entertained us for our money with such provisions and refreshings as those parts afforded.

By this time, the King of the country had notice of our being there, and, as I suppose, grew suspicious of us; not having all that while by any message, made him acquainted with our intent and purpose in coming. Thereupon he despatched down a *Dissauva* or general with his army to us. Who immediately sent a messenger on board to acquaint the Captain with his coming and desired him to come ashore to him; pretending to have a letter to him from the King. We saluted the message with the firing of guns, and my father the Captain, ordered me with Master JOHN LOVELAND, merchant [*supercargo*] of the ship, to go on shore and wait upon him.

When we were come before him; he demanded "Who we were?" and "How long we should stay?" We told him, "We were English," and "Not to stay above twenty or thirty days:" and desired permission to trade in his Majesty's port. His answer was, "The King was glad to hear that the

English were come to his country, and had commanded him to assist us as we should desire; and had sent a letter to be delivered to none but to the Captain himself."

We were then some twelve miles from the seaside. Our reply was, "That the Captain could not leave his ship to come so far; but if he pleased to come down to the seaside himself, the Captain would immediately wait upon him to receive the letter." Upon which, the Dissauva desired us to stay that day; and on the morrow, he would go down with us: which being a small request; we, unwilling to displease him, consented to.

The same day at evening, the Dissauva sent two of his chief captains to the house where we lay, to tell us "That he was sending a present to the Captain, and if we pleased we might send a letter to him: that he would send the present in the night; and himself, with us, follow the next morning." At which, we began to suspect, and accordingly concluded to write and advise the Captain not to adventure himself nor any other on shore, till he saw us. We having written a letter to this purpose, they took it and went away; but never delivered it.

The next morning, the present (which was cattle, fruit, &c.) was brought to the seaside and delivered to the Captain; the messengers telling him withal, that we were upon the way coming down with the Dissauva, who desired his company on shore, against his coming; having a letter from the King to deliver into his own hand. Hereupon the Captain mistrusting nothing, came up with his boat into a small river; and being come ashore, sat down under a tamarind tree,* waiting for the Dissauva and us. In which time, the native soldiers privately surrounded him and his men having no arms with them: and so he was seized on, and seven men with him; yet without any violence or plundering them of

* Sir JAMES EMERSON TENNENT, K.C.G., in a tour through the northern forests of Ceylon in February 1848, thus—

"At Cottiar, . . . we halted by the identical tamarind tree, under which, two centuries before, Captain ROBERT KNOX—the gentlest of historians, and the meekest of captives—was betrayed by the Kandyans; and thence carried into their hills: to be detained an inoffensive prisoner, from boyhood to grey hairs. But to that captivity, we are indebted for the most faithful and life-like portraiture that was ever drawn of a semi-civilised, but remarkable people."—*Ceylon*. ii. 478. *Ed.* 1859.

anything. And then they brought them up unto us, carrying the Captain in a hammock upon their shoulders.

The next day after, the long boat's crew not knowing what had happened, came ashore to cut a tree to make cheeks for the mainmast; and were made prisoners after the same manner, though with more violence. For they being rough and making resistance, were bound with withes; and so were led away till they came where the people got ropes. Which when our men saw brought to them, they were not a little affrighted; for being already bound, they concluded there could be no other use for those ropes but to hang them. But the true use of them was to bind them faster, fearing lest the withes might break; and so they were brought up farther into the country; but afterwards being become more tame, they were loosed. They would not adventure to bring them to us, but quartered them in another house, though in the same town: where without leave, we could not see one another. The house where they kept the Captain and us, was all hanged with white calico; which is the greatest honour they can show to any: but the house wherein the other men were, that were brought up after us, was not. They gave us also as good entertainment as the country afforded.

Having thus taken both our boats and eighteen men of us; their next care was, fearing lest the ship should be gone, to secure her. Therefore to bring this about, the Dissauva told the Captain that the reason of this their detainment was that the King intended to send letters and a present to the English nation by him; and therefore that the ship must not go away till the King was ready to send his messenger and message: and thereupon desired the Captain to send on board to order her stay, and—it being not safe for her to ride in the bay, lest the Dutch might come and fire her—that he should take order for her bringing up into the river. Which advice of his, the Captain approved not of; but concealing his dislike to it, replied "that unless he could send two of his own men on board with his letter and order, those in the ship would not obey him, but speedily would be gone with the ship." Which he, rather than he would run the hazard of the ship's departing, granted: imagining that the Captain would order the ship to be brought up into the river, as he had advised; though the Captain intended to make another use of this message.

Upon which, the Captain sent two of his men, some Indians accompanying them, in a canoe to the ship; the Captain ordering them, when they were aboard not to abuse the Indians, but to entertain them very kindly: and afterwards that, setting them ashore, they should keep the canoe to themselves, instead of our two boats which they had gotten from us; and to secure the ship, and wait till further orders.

These two men stayed on board, and came not back again. This, together with the ship's not coming up, displeased the Dissauva; and he demanded of the Captain the reason thereof. His answer was, "That being detained on shore, the men on board would not obey his command."

Upon this, some days after, the Dissauva bid the Captain send his son with orders to those aboard that the ship might be brought into the river; but provided that he would be security for my return: which he promised he would. His order to me was, "to see the top chains put upon the cables, and the guns shotted [*loaded*]; and to tell Master JOHN BURFORD Chief Mate, and all the rest, as they valued their lives and liberties, to keep a watch; and not to suffer any boat to come near, after it was dark: and charged me upon his blessing, and as I should answer it at the Great Day, not to leave him in this condition; but to return to him again." Upon which I solemnly vowed, according to my duty, to be his obedient son.

So, having seen all done according to his appointment, I wrote a letter in the name of the company to clear my father and myself, to this effect, "That they would not obey the Captain, nor any other in this matter; but were resolved to stand upon their own defence." To which they all set their hands. Which done, according to my promise and duty, I returned again; and delivered the letter to the Dissauva, who was thereby answered: and afterwards urged the Captain no more in that matter, but gave him leave at his pleasure to write for what he pleased to have brought to him from the ship; still pretending the King's order to release us was not yet, but would suddenly come.

And so we remained expecting it, about two months; being entertained, as formerly, with the best diet and accommodation of the country.

Having continued thus long in suspense, and the time and the year spending [*passing away*] for the ship to proceed on her voyage to some other place; and our condition being, as we feared and afterwards found to be, the beginning of a sad captivity: the Captain sent orders to Master JOHN BURFORD to take the charge of the ship upon him, and to set sail for Porto Nova, whence we came; and there to follow the [Madras] Agent's order.

If any inquire what became of the cloth of our lading, which we brought thither; they only took an account to see what it was, and so left it where and as it was before: and there it remained until both house and goods rotted away, as the people of the same town informed me afterwards.

I impute the main reason of our surprise to our neglect, viz., in not sending a letter and present to the King at our first coming: who looking upon himself as a great monarch, as he is indeed, requires to be treated with suitable state.

Thus were sixteen of us left to the mercy of those barbarians: the names of which are as follows. The Captain, Master JOHN LOVELAND, JOHN GREGORY, CHARLES BEARD, ROGER GOLD, STEPHEN RUTLAND, NICHOLAS MULLINS, FRANCIS CRUTCH, JOHN BERRY, RALPH KNIGHT, PETER WINN, WILLIAM HUBBARD, ANTONY EMERY, RICHARD VARNHAM, GEORGE SMITH, and myself. Though our hearts were very heavy, seeing ourselves betrayed into so sad a condition, to be forced to dwell among those that knew not GOD nor His laws: yet so great was the mercy of our gracious GOD, that He gave us favour in the sight of this people: insomuch that we lived far better than we could have expected, being prisoners or rather captives in the hands of the heathen; from whom we could have looked for nothing but very severe usage.

The ship being gone, the King sent to call the Dissauva speedily to him; who, upon this order, immediately marched away with his army; leaving us where we were. But concerning us, there was no order at all.

CHAPTER II.

How we were carried up into the country, and disposed of there: and of the sickness, sorrow and death of the Captain.

THE Dissauva with his men, being gone; the people of the town were appointed to guard and secure us until further orders. But they carried us some six miles higher into the country; and would not yet adventure to bring the long boat's crew unto us, but kept them by themselves in another town: fearing lest we might make an escape; as certainly we would have attempted it, had they not removed us.

There was a small Moor's vessel, which lay in the river; which they had seized on about this time, as we supposed they would have done by our ship, if they could have caught her there. This vessel had some forty men belonging to her; who were not made prisoners as we were, but yet lay in the same town. With those, we had concluded that they should furnish us with arms: and, in the night, all together to march down and get on board their vessel; and so make our escape. But being prevented in this design by our departure, we were fain to lie at their mercy.

In our new quarters, our entertainment proved as good as formerly: and indeed there was this to mitigate our misery; that the people were courteous to us, and seemed to pity us. For there is a great difference between the people inhabiting the high lands or mountains of Kandy, and those of the low lands where we now were placed; who are of a kinder nature by far, than the other. For these countries beneath the mountains formerly were in subjection to the Portuguese; whereby they have been exercised and acquainted with the customs and manners of Christian people: which pleasing them far better than their own, have begot and bred in them a kind of love and affection towards strangers; being apt to show pity and compassion on them in their distress. And you shall hear them oftentimes upbraiding the highlanders for their insolent and rude behaviour.

It was a very sad condition whilst we were all together; yet hitherto each other's company lessened our sufferings, and was some comfort, that we might condole one another. But now it came to pass that we must be separated and placed asunder, one in a village; where we could have none to confer withal or look upon, but the horrible black faces of our heathen enemies, and not understand one word of their language neither. This was a great addition to our grief. Yet GOD was so merciful to us, as not to suffer them to part my father and I.

For it was some sixteen days after our last remove, the King was pleased to send a captain with soldiers to bring us up into the country; who brought us and the other men taken in the long boat together: which was a heavy meeting; being then, as we well saw, to be carried captives into the mountains. That night we supped together; and the next morning changed our condition into real captivity. Howbeit they gave us many comfortable promises, which we believed not; as "That the King's intent was not to keep us any longer than till another ship came to carry us away." Although we had but very little to carry, GOD knows; yet they appointed men to carry the clothes that belonged to the Captain and Officers. We still expected they would plunder us of our clothes, having nothing else to be plundered of: but the Cingalese captain told us, that the King had given order that none should take the value of a thread from us; which indeed they did not.

As they brought us up, they were very tender of us; as not to tire us with travelling, bidding us go no faster than we would ourselves. This kindness did somewhat comfort us. The way was plain and easy to travel, through great woods, so that we walked as in an arbour; but desolate of inhabitants: so that for four or five nights we lay on the ground, with boughs of trees only over our heads. And of victuals, twice a day they gave us as much as we could eat; that is, of rice, salt fish, dried flesh: and sometimes they would shoot deer, and find honey in the trees; a good part of which they always brought unto us. And drink we could not want; there being rivers and puddles full of water, as we travelled along.

But when we came out of the woods amongst inhabitants, and were led into their towns; they brought us victuals ready dressed after their fashion, viz.: rice boiled in water, and three other sorts of food, whereof one was flesh and the other two herbs or such like things that grow in their country; and all kinds of ripe fruit: which we liked very well and fed heartily upon. Our entertainment all along was at the charge of the country, so we fed like soldiers upon free quarters. Yet I think we gave them good content for all the charge we put them to; which was to have the satisfaction of seeing us eat, sitting on mats upon the ground in their yards to the public view of all beholders: who greatly admired us; having never seen, nor scarce heard of Englishmen before. It was also great entertainment to them to observe our manner of eating with spoons, which some of us had; and that we could not take the rice up in our hands and put it to our mouths without spilling, as they do; nor gaped and poured the water into our mouths out of pots, according to their country's fashion. Thus at every town where we came; they used both young and old in great companies, to stare upon us.

Being thus brought up altogether somewhat near to the city of Kandy; now came an order from the King to separate us, and to place us one in a town. Which then seemed to us to be very hard; but it was for the convenience of getting food, being quartered upon the country at their charge.

The Captain, Master JOHN LOVELAND, myself and JOHN GREGORY were parted from the rest, and brought nearer to the city; to be ready when the King should send for us: all the rest were placed one in a town, according to the aforesaid order. Special command also was given from the King that we all should be well entertained; and according to the country's fare, we had no cause to complain. We four were thus kept together some two months, faring well all the while.

But the King minding us not, order came from the great men in court to place us in towns, as the rest were; only my father and I were still permitted to be together: and a great charge given to use us well. And indeed twice a day, we had brought unto us as good fare as the country afforded. All the rest had not their provisions brought to them, as we had; but went to eat from house to house, each house taking its turn.

On the 16th of September 1660, my father and I were placed in a town called Bonder Coswat. The situation was very pleasing and commodious, lying about thirty miles to the northward of the city of Kandy, in the country called Hotkorle [? *Hewarrisse Korle*], and distant from the rest of our people a full day's journey. We were removed hither from another town nearer to the city of Kandy, where the nobles at Court supposing that the King would call for us, had placed us to have us ready.

Being thus brought to Bonder Coswat; the people put it to our choice, which house we would have to reside in. The country being hot, and their houses dark and dirty; my father chose an open house; having only a roof, but no walls: wherein they placed a cot or bedstead with a mat only upon it for him, which in their account is an extraordinary lodging; and for me, a mat on the ground.

Money at that time was very low with us. For although we wanted not for opportunity to send for what we would have brought unto us from the ship; yet fearing we should be plundered of it, we sent not for anything save a pillow for my father. For we held it a point without dispute, that they that made prisoners of our bodies would not spare to take our goods: my father also alleging that he had rather his children at home should enjoy them.

But to make amends for that; we had our provisions brought us without money, and that twice a day, so much as we could eat and as good as their country yielded. To wit, a pot of good rice, and three dishes of such things as with them are accounted good cheer; one always either flesh, fish or eggs, but not overmuch of this dish; the other dishes, herbs, pumpkins or such like, one of which was always made sour.

The first year that we were brought to this town; this part of the land was extraordinarily sickly with agues and fevers, whereof many people died: insomuch that many times we were forced to remain an hungry; there being none well enough either to boil or bring victuals unto us.

We had with us a *Practice of Piety*, and Master ROGER'S *Seven Treatises* called *The Practice of Christianity*. With which companions we did frequently discourse; and in the cool of the evening walked abroad in the field for a refreshing, being tired with being all day in our house or prison.

This course lasted until GOD was pleased to visit us both with the country's sickness, ague and fever. The sight of my father's misery was far more grievous unto me than the sense of my own; that I must be a spectator of his affliction, and not in any way able to help him. And the sight of me so far augmented his grief, that he would often say "What have I done, when I charged you to come ashore to me again? Your dutifulness to me hath brought you to be a captive. I am old and cannot long hold out, but you may live to see many days of sorrow; if the mercy of GOD do not prevent it. But my prayers to GOD for you shall not be wanting; that for this cause, he would visit you with his mercy and bestow on you a blessing."

My father's ague lasted not long; but deep grief daily more and more increased upon him; which so overwhelmed even his very heart, that with many a bitter sigh, he used to utter these words, "These many years, even from my youth, have I used the seas; in which time the Lord GOD hath delivered me from a multitude of dangers"—rehearsing to me what great dangers he had been in in the Straits of Gibraltar by the Turks and by other enemies, and also in many other places too large here to insert; and always how merciful GOD was to him in delivering him out of them all —"so that he never knew what it was to be in the hands of an enemy: but now, in his old age, when his head was grown grey, to be a captive to the heathen, and to leave his bones in the eastern parts of the world: when it was his hope and intention, if GOD had permitted him to finish this voyage, to spend and end the residue of his days at home with his children in his native country; and so to settle me in the ship in his stead. The thoughts of these things did ever break his heart."

Upwards of three months, my father lay in this manner upon his bed; having only under him a mat and the carpet he sat upon in the boat when he came ashore, and a small quilt I had to cover him withal. And I had only a mat upon the ground, and a pillow to lay on; and nothing to cover me but the clothes on my back: but when I was cold and that my ague came upon me, I used to make a fire; wood costing nothing but the fetching.

We had a black boy [? *a Madrassee*] that my father brought from Porto Nova to attend upon him: who seeing his master to be a prisoner in the hands of the people of his complexion, would not now obey his command further than what agreed unto his own humour: neither was it then, as we thought, in our power to compel or make him; but that was our ignorance.

As for me, my ague now came to a settled course, that is, once in three days, and so continued for sixteen months' time.

There appearing now to us no probability, whereupon to build any hopes of liberty: the sense of it struck my father into such an agony and strong passion of grief that once, I well remember, in nine days' time nothing came into his mouth but cold water; neither did he in three months together, ever rise up out of his bed but when the course of nature required it: always groaning and sighing in a most piteous manner, which for me to hear and see come from my dear father, myself also in the same condition, did almost break my heart. But then I felt that doctrine most true, which I had read out of Master ROGERS's book, "That GOD is most sweet; when the world is most bitter."

In this manner my father lay until the 9th of February 1661: by which time he was consumed to an anatomy [*reduced to a skeleton*], having nothing left but skin to cover his bones. Yet he would often say, "that the very sound of liberty would so revive him, that it would put strength into his limbs." But it was not the will of Him, to whom we say "Thy will be done" to have it so.

The evening before his death, he called me to come near his bedside, and to sit down by him; at which time I had also a strong fever upon me. This done, he told me, "That he sensibly felt his life departing from him, and was assured that this night GOD would deliver him out of his captivity: and that he never thought, in all his lifetime, that death could be so easy and welcome to any man as GOD had made it to be to him, and the joys he now felt in himself he wanted utterance to express to me." He told me "These were the last words that ever he should speak to me, and bade me well to regard and to be sure to remember them, and tell them to my brother and sister, if it pleased GOD, as he hoped it would, to bring us together in England, where I should find all things settled to my contentation:" relating unto me after what manner he had settled his estate by letters, which he sent from Kottiaar.

"In the first place, and above all; he charged me to serve GOD, and with a circumspect care to walk in His ways; and then," he said, "GOD would bless me and prosper me." And next, he bade me, "have a care of my brother and sister." And lastly, he gave me "a special charge to beware of strong drink and lewd company; which, as by experience many had found, would change me into another man, so that I should not be myself." "It deeply grieved him," he said, "to see me in captivity in the prime of my years, and so much the more because I had chosen rather to suffer captivity with him than to disobey his command; which now he was heartily sorry for, that he had so commanded me: but bade me not repent of obeying the command of my father, seeing for this very thing," he said, "GOD would bless me," and bade me "be assured of it, which he doubted not of, namely, that GOD Almighty would deliver me." Which, at that time, I could not tell how to conceive of, seeing but little sign of any such matter. But blessed be the Name of my most precious GOD, who hath so bountifully sustained me ever since in the land of my captivity, and preserved me alike to see my deceased father's word fulfilled! And truly I was so far from repenting that I had obeyed the command of my father, and performed the oath and promise I made unto him upon it; that it rather rejoiced me to see that GOD had given me so much grace.

But though it was a trouble to him, that by his means, I was thus made a captive; yet "it was a great comfort to him," he said, "to have his own son sit by him on his death-bed, and by his hands to be buried; whereas otherwise he could expect no other but to be eaten by dogs or wild beasts." Then he gave me order concerning his burial, "That having no winding sheet, I should pull his shirt over his head and slip his breeches over his feet, and so wrap him up in the mat he laid upon." And then he ceased speaking, and fell into a slumber. This was about eight or nine o'clock in the evening: and about two or three in the morning he gave up the ghost, February 9th 1660; being very sensible unto the very instant of his departure.

According to his own appointment; with my own hands, I wrapped him up ready for the grave: myself being very sick and weak; and, as I thought, ready to follow after him.

Having none but the black boy, I bade him ask the people of the town for help to carry my father to the grave; because I could not understand their language: who immediately brought forth a great rope they used to tie their cattle withal, therewith to drag him by the neck into the woods; saying "that they could afford me no other help, unless I would pay for it." This insolency of the heathen grieved me much to see; neither could I, with the boy alone, do what was necessary for his burial, though we had been able to carry the corpse: having not wherewithal to dig a grave, and the ground being very dry and hard. Yet it was some comfort to me, that I had so much ability as to hire one to help; which at first I would not have spared to have done, had I known their meaning.

By this means, I thank God, in so decent a manner as our present condition would permit, I laid my father's body in the grave; most of which I digged with my own hands: the place being in a wood on the north side of a corn field, where heretofore we had used often to walk, going up to Handapoul [? *Handepoli*]. That division, as I have said, being called Bonder Coswat, because formerly it had belonged to the revenues or jointure of the Queen: *Bonder* implying something relating to the King. It lies towards the north-west of the middle of the island, in the county of Hotkorle.

Thus was I left desolate, sick, and in captivity; having no earthly comforter; none but only He who looks down from heaven to hear the groaning of the prisoners; and to show himself a Father to the fatherless, and a present help to them that have no helper.

The news of my father's death being carried to Court; presently two messengers were sent from thence to see me, and to know of me how and in what manner my father died; and what he had left? Which was a gold ring, a pagoda [= 6s. *in present value*], some two or three dollars, and a few old clothes; GOD knows but a very little: yet it scared me not a little, fearing they would take it away from me, and my want being so great: but they had no such order or intent. But the chief occasion of their coming was to renew the former order unto the people of that town: that they should be kind to me; and give me good victuals, lest I might die also, as my father had done. So for a while I had better entertainment than formerly.

CHAPTER III.

How I lived after my father's death: and of the condition of the rest of the English, and how it fared with them. And of our interview.

I STILL remained where I was before; having none but the black boy and my ague to bear me company. Never found I more pleasure in reading, meditating and praying than now: for there was nothing else could administer to me any comfort; neither had I any other business to be occupied about. I had read my two books so often over, that I had them almost by heart. For my custom was after dinner, to take a book and go into the fields and sit under a tree; reading and meditating until evening: except the day when my ague came, for then I could scarce hold up my head. Often have I prayed as ELIJAH under the juniper tree, that GOD would take away my life; for it was a burden to me.

At length it pleased GOD that my ague began to be a little moderate; and so, by degrees, it wore away: after it had held me sixteen months.

Provisions falling short with me, though rice, I thank GOD, I never wanted, and money also growing low: as well to help out a meal as for recreation; sometimes I went with an angle to catch small fish in the brooks, the aforesaid boy being with me.

It chanced, as I was fishing, an old man passed by; and seeing me, asked of my boy, "if I could read in a book?" He answered "Yes." "The reason I ask," said the old man, "is because I have one I got when the Portuguese lost Colombo; and if your master please to buy it, I will sell it him." Which when I heard of, I bade my boy go to his house with him, which was not far off, and bring it to me to see it; making no great account of the matter, supposing it might be some Portuguese book.

The boy having formerly served the English, knew the

book; and as soon as he had got it in his hand, came running with it, calling out to me "It is a Bible." It startled me to hear him mention the name of a "Bible:" for I neither had one, nor scarcely could ever think to see one. Upon which, I flung down my angle, and went to meet him. The first place the book opened in, after I took it in my hand, was the sixteenth chapter of the Acts, and the first place my eye pitched on, was the 30th and 31st verses, where the gaoler asked St. PAUL "What must I do to be saved? And he answered saying, Believe in the Lord JESUS CHRIST, and thou shalt be saved and thine house."

The sight of this book so rejoiced me, and affrighted me together; that I cannot say which passion was greater, the Joy for that I had got sight of a Bible, or the Fear that I had not enough to buy it, having then but one pagoda in the world: which I willingly would have given for it, but my boy dissuaded me from giving so much, alleging my necessity for money many other ways, and undertaking to procure the book for a far meaner price; provided I would seem to slight it in the sight of the old man. This counsel after I considered, I approved of, my urgent necessities earnestly craving, and my ability being but very small to relieve the same: and however, I thought, I could give my piece of gold at the last cast, if other means should fail.

I hope the readers will excuse me, that I hold them so long upon this single passage; for it did so affect me then, that I cannot lightly pass it over as often as I think of it, or have occasion to mention it. The sight indeed of this Bible so overjoyed me, as if an angel had spoken to me from heaven. To see that my gracious GOD had prepared such an extraordinary blessing for me, which I did, and ever shall look upon as miraculous: to bring unto me a Bible in my own native language; and that in such a remote part of the world where His name was not so much as known, and where any Englishman was never known to have been before. I looked upon it as somewhat of the same nature with the Ten Commandments He had given the Israelites out of heaven. It being the thing for want whereof I had so often mourned, nay and shed tears too; and than the enjoyment whereof, there could be no greater joy in the world to me.

Upon the sight of it I left off fishing; GOD having brought

a fish to me that I longed for: and now how to get it and enjoy the same, all the powers of my soul were employed. I gave GOD hearty thanks that He had brought it so near me, and most earnestly prayed that He would bestow it on me. Now it being well towards evening, and not having wherewithal to buy it about me, I departed home; telling the old man that in the morning I would send my boy to buy it of him.

All that night I could take no rest for thinking on it, fearing lest I might be disappointed of it. In the morning, as soon as it was day, I sent the boy with a knit cap he had made for me to buy the book, praying in my heart for good success: which it pleased GOD to grant. For that cap purchased it, and the boy brought it to me to my great joy; which did not a little comfort me in all my afflictions.

Having said all this concerning my father and myself, it will now be time to think of the rest of our poor countrymen, and to see what is become of them.

They were carried into the county of Hotterakorle, westward from the city of Kandy; and placed singly according to the King's order aforesaid, some four, some six miles distant one from the other. It was the King's command concerning them that the people should give them victuals, and look after them: so they carried each man from house to house to eat, as their turns came to give them victuals: and where they supped, there they lodged that night. Their bedding was only a mat upon the ground.

They knew not that they were so near to one another a great while, till at length Almighty GOD was pleased by their grief and heaviness to move those heathen to pity and take compassion on them; so that they did bring some of them to one another. Which joy was but abortive, for no sooner did they begin to feel the comfort of one another's company; but immediately their keepers called upon them to go from whence they came, fearing they might consult and run away, although Colombo, the nearest port they could fly to, was above two days' journey from them. But as it is with wild beasts beginning to grow tame, their liberty increaseth; so it happened to our men. So that at length, they might go and see one another at their pleasures; and were less and less watched and regarded: and seeing they did not attempt to run away; they made no matter of it, if they stayed two or three days one with the other.

They all wondered much to see themselves in this condition, to be kept only to eat; and the people of the country giving it unto them, daily expecting when they would put them to work, which they never did nor dared to do. For the King's order was to feed them well only, and to look after them; until he pleased to send for them.

This, after some time, made the Englishmen change their minds, and not to think themselves slaves any more; but the inhabitants of the land to be their servants, in that they laboured to sustain them: which made them to begin to domineer, and would not be content, unless they had such victuals as pleased them; and oftentimes used to throw the pots victuals and all, at their heads that brought them, which they patiently would bear.

And as they lived here longer, they knew better what privileges they had in belonging unto the King; and being maintained by virtue of his command. And their privileges they made use of to no purpose, as I shall relate an instance or two by and by, and showed their English metal.

Victuals were the only thing allowed to them, but no clothes. By this time the clothes they had were almost worn out. This put them to a study what course to take to procure more, when those on their backs were gone. The readiest way that they could devise was this, that whereas they used to take their victuals brought to them ready dressed, they should now take them raw; and so to pinch somewhat out of their bellies to save to buy clothes for their backs. And so accordingly they concluded to do, and by the favour that GOD gave them in the sight of the people, by alleging the innocency of their cause and the extremity of their present condition, having not the least ability to help or relieve themselves; they consented to give them two measures of rice a day each man, one of which is as much as any man can eat in a day, so that the other was to serve for advance towards clothes. For besides rice, they gave them to eat with it, salt, pepper, limes, herbs, pumpkins, cocoa nuts, flesh (a little): these, and such like things, were their constant fare.

And thus they made a shift to live for some years, until

some of them had an insight in knitting caps, by whom all afterwards learned: and it proved to be the chief means and help we all had to relieve our wants. The ordinary price we sold these caps for was ninepence apiece, in value of English money; the thread standing us in about three pence. But at length—we plying hard our new learned trade—caps began to abound, and trading grew dead, so that we could not sell them at the former price; which brought several of our nation to great want.

The English began now to pluck up their hearts; and though they were entered into a new condition, they kept their old spirits: especially considering they were the King's men, and quartered by his special order, upon the people.

When they had obtained to have their allowance raw, if any brought them not their full due, they would go in and plunder their houses of such goods as they found there: and keep them until they came and brought them their complete allowance to redeem their goods back again.

Some of our Englishmen have proceeded further yet. One, for example, went to buy pots of a potter; who, because he [*the potter*] would not let him have them at his own price, fell to a quarrel; in which the Englishman met with some blows: which he complained of to the magistrate, as being a person that belonged unto the King, and therefore claimed better usage. And the magistrate condemned the potter as guilty in lifting up his hand against him; and sent some of his soldiers to bind him, and then bade the Englishman go and content himself by paying him in the same coin again as he had served our countryman, which he did until he was satisfied: and moreover, ordered him to take the pots he came to buy and pay nothing. But the law was not so satisfied neither: for the soldiers lay on many blows besides.

Another time, at a certain feast, as they were drinking and wanting wine, they sent money to buy more; but the seller refused to give it them for their money: which they took so heinously, that they unanimously concluded to go and take it by force. Away they went, each man with a staff in his hand, and entered the house and began to drink: which the people, not liking of, gathered their forces together, and by blows began to resist them. But the Englishmen bravely behaved themselves, and broke several of their pates: who, with the blood about their ears, went to the city of Kandy to complain to the great men. They demanded of them, "if they had ever sold them wine before." They answered "Yes." They asked them again, "Why then did they refuse to sell to them now?" and that they were well served by the English for denying them drink for their money: and so sent them away, laughing at them. Our men got two or three black and blue blows; but they came home with their bellies full of drink for their pains.

But to return unto myself. It was a full year after my father died, before I had sight of any of my countrymen and fellow prisoners. Then JOHN GREGORY, with much ado, obtained leave to come and see me; which did exceedingly rejoice me. For a great satisfaction it was, both to see a countryman, and also to hear of the welfare of the rest. But he could not be permitted to stay with me above one day. Until then, I knew not punctually [*exactly*] where the rest of my countrymen were: but having heard that they were within a day's journey of me, I never ceased importuning the people of the town where I dwelt, to let me go and see them: which though very loth, yet at last they granted.

Being arrived at the nearest Englishman's house, I was joyfully received; and the next day, he went and called some of the rest of our countrymen that were near. So that there were some seven or eight of us met together.

We gave GOD thanks for His great mercies towards us; being then, as we did confess, in a far better condition than we could have expected. They were now no more like the prisoners I left them: but were become housekeepers and knitters of caps; and had changed their habit from breeches to clouts [*clothes*] like the Cingalese. They entertained me with very good cheer in their houses, beyond what I did expect.

My money, at the same time, being almost gone; and clothes in the same condition: it was high time for me now to take some course in hand to get more. Therefore I took some advice with them about knitting, my boy having skill therein. Likewise they advised me to take my victuals raw wherein they found great profit. For all this while there being no signs of releasing us, it concerned me now to bethink myself how I should live for the future. For neither had I any more than my countrymen any allowance for clothes, but for victuals only.

Having stayed here some two or three days; we did take leave of one another, hoping to see one another oftener: since we now knew each other's habitations: and I departed to my house, having a keeper with me.

By this time, I began to speak the language of the country, whereby I was enabled the better to speak my mind unto the people that brought me my victuals; which was, henceforth not to boil my rice but to bring it raw, according to the quantity that the other Englishmen had. This occasioned a great deal of disputing and reasoning between us. They alleged "that I was not as they, being the Captain's son and they but his servants: and therefore that it was ordered by the great men at Court that my victuals should be daily brought unto me; whereas they went always from house to house for theirs. Neither was it fitting for me," they said, "to employ myself in such an inferior office as to dress my own meat, being a man that the King had notice of by name; and very suddenly before I should be aware of it, would send for me into his presence; where I should be highly promoted to some place of honour. In the mean time," they told me, as pretending to give me good counsel, "that it was more for my credit and reputation to have my provisions brought unto me ready dressed as they were before."

Although I was yet but a novice in the country, and knew not much of the people; yet plain reason told me that it was not so much for my good and credit that they pleaded, as for their own benefit: wherefore I returned them this answer, "That if, as they said, I was greater in quality than the rest, and so held in their estimation; it would be but reason to demand a greater allowance; whereas I desired no more than the other Englishmen had: and as for the toil and trouble in dressing of it, that would be none to me, for my boy had nothing else to do." And then I alleged several inconveniences in bringing my victuals ready boiled: as first, that it was not dressed according to my diet; and many times not brought in due season, so that I could not eat when I was an hungry; and the last and chief reason was, that I might save a little to serve my necessity for clothing; and rather than want clothes for my back, I must pinch a little out of my belly; and so both go share and share alike.

And so at length, thanks be to GOD, I obtained, though with much ado, to get two measures of rice per diem for myself, and one for my boy; also cocoa nuts, pumpkins, herbs, limes, and such like enough; besides pepper and salt; and sometimes hens, eggs, or flesh: rice being the main thing they stand upon, for of other things they refuse not to give what they have.

Now having settled all business about my allowance, my next concern was to look after a house more convenient; for my present one was too small to dress my victuals in and sleep in too. Thereabouts was a garden of cocoa-nut trees belonging to the King, and a pleasant situation. This place I made choice of to build me a house in: and discovering my desire to the people; they consented, and came and built it for me. But before it was finished, their occasions called them away; but my boy and I made an end of it, and whitened [*whitewashed*] the walls with lime, according to my own country's fashion. But in doing this, I committed a capital offence: for none may white[wash] their houses with lime, that being peculiar to the royal houses and temples: but, being a stranger, nothing was made of it, because I did it in ignorance. Had it been a native that had so done, it is most probable that it would have cost him his head, or at the least a great fine.

Being settled in my new house, I began to keep hogs and hens; which, by GOD's blessing, throve very well with me, and were a great help unto me. I had also a great benefit by living in this garden. For all the cocoa nuts that fell down, they gave me; which afforded me oil to burn in the lamp, and also to fry my meat in: which oil being new, is but little inferior to this country's butter. Now I learned to knit caps, which skill I quickly attained unto; and, by GOD's blessing upon the same, I obtained great help and relief thereby.

In this manner we all lived: seeing but very little sign that we might build upon, to look for liberty. The chief of our hopes of it was that in process of time, when we were better acquainted, we might run away: which some of our people attempted to do too soon, before they knew well which way to go, and were taken by the inhabitants. For it is the custom of the Cingalese to suspect all white people they meet travelling in the country to be runaways, and to examine them: and if they cannot give satisfactory answers, they will lay hold of them and carry them back unto the city [of Kandy]; where they will keep them prisoners under a guard of soldiers, in an open house like a barn, with a little victuals sometimes, and sometimes with none at all. Where they have no other remedy to help themselves but begging: and in this condition, they may lie perhaps for their lifetime; being so kept for a spectacle unto the people.

Though the common way whereby the King gratifies such as catch runaways and bring them up [to the city], is not over acceptable. For they are appointed to feed and watch them, until he calls for them to be brought before him; at which time, his promise is bountifully to reward them. But these promises I never knew performed: neither doth he perhaps ever think of it after. For when the King is made acquainted with the matter, the men that have brought up the prisoner are in a manner as bad prisoners themselves; not daring to go home to their houses, without his leave: but there they must remain. After some years' stay, the common manner is for them to give a fee unto the governor of the country, and he will license them to go home; which they must be contented with, instead of the promised reward.

CHAPTER IV.

Concerning some other Englishmen detained in that country.

IN the same captivity with ourselves on this island was another company of Englishmen, who were taken about a year and a half before us, viz.: in the year 1658. They were thirteen in number, whose names were as follows, viz.:—Master WILLIAM VASSAL, JOHN MERGINSON, THOMAS MARCH, THOMAS KIRBY, RICHARD JELF, GAMALIEL GARDNER, WILLIAM DAY, THOMAS STAPLETON, HENRY MAN, HUGH SMART, DANIEL HOLSTEIN an Hamburgher, JAMES GONY and HENRY BINGHAM.

The occasion of their seizure was thus. The ship these men belonged to, was the *Persia Merchant*, Captain FRANCIS JOHNSON Commander; which was lost upon the Maldive islands: but they escaped in their boats, and passing along by this land went on shore to recruit and buy provisions; and so were taken. The Cingalese that took them, plundered them of what they had, except their clothes. Yet one of them, JOHN MERGINSON by name, having cunningly hid his money about him, saved it from the heathen: but from his own countrymen he could not; some of them knowing of it, set upon him and robbed him of it. But it did them little good, for the King hearing of it, sent and robbed the robbers.

These men thus seized, were carried up before the King, of whom he demanded, "whether the English had wars with the Hollanders?" They answered, "No." "Or if the English could beat them?" They answered, "They could, and had done it lately." Then he gave order to give them all some clothes; and to Master WILLIAM VASSAL, being the chief of them, a double portion. And out of them, he made choice of two lads, whom afterwards he sent and took into his Court. Their honours and their ends we shall see by and by.

They were all placed in the city of Kandy, and each of

them had a new mat given them to sleep on, and their diet was victuals dressed and brought them, twice a day, from the King's own palace. They had clothes also distributed to them at another time. So that these men had the advantage of us: for we neither had mats nor clothes, nor had the honour of being ever brought into the King's presence.

This civil reception upon their first coming up into the city put the *Persia Merchant* men in hope that the King would give them their liberty. There was at that time an old Portuguese father, Padre VERGONSE by name, living in the city. With him they discoursed concerning the probability of their liberty, and that the favours the King had shown them seemed to be good signs of it: but he told them the plain truth, that it was not customary there to release white men. For saying which, they railed on him; calling him "Popish dog" and "Jesuitical rogue," supposing he spoke as he wished it might be: but afterwards, to their grief, they found it to be true as he told them.

Their entertainment was excellently good according to the poor condition of the country: but they thought it otherwise, very mean; and not according to the King's order. Therefore that the King might be informed how they were abused, each man took the limb of a hen in his hand, and they marched rank and file, in order, through the streets, with it in their hands to the Court; as a sign to the great men, whereby they might see how illy [*badly*] they were served: thinking hereby the King might come to hear of their misusage, and so they might have orders to be fed better afterwards. But this proved sport to the noblemen who knew well the fare of the country: they laughing at their ignorance, to complain where they had so little cause. And indeed afterwards, they themselves laughed at this action of theirs, and were half ashamed of it; when they came to a better understanding of the nature of the country's diet.

Yet notwithstanding, being not used to such short commons of flesh, though they had rice in abundance, and having no money to buy more; they had a desire to kill some cows, that they might eat their bellies full of beef: but made it somewhat a point of conscience, whether it might be lawful or not to take them without leave. Upon which they applied themselves to the old father aforesaid, desiring him to solve this case of conscience: who was very ready to give them a dispensation; and told them, "that forasmuch as the Cingalese were their enemies and had taken their bodies, it was very lawful for them to satisfy their bodies with their goods." And the better to animate them in this design, he bade them bring him a piece that he might partake with them. So being encouraged by the old father, they went on boldly in their intended business.

Now if you would have an account of the mettle and manfulness of these men, as you have already had a taste of those of ours; take this passage. The Jak fruit the King's officers often gather wheresoever it grows, and give it to the King's elephants; and they may gather it in any man's grounds without the owner's leave, being for the King's use. Now these Englishmen were appointed to dwell in a house that formerly belonged unto a nobleman, whom the King had cut off, and seized upon it. In the ground belonging to this house stood a Jak tree full of fruit. Some of the King's men came thither to gather some to feed the elephants: but although the English had free liberty to gather what they could eat or desire; yet they would permit none but themselves to meddle with them, but took the officers by the shoulders and turned them out of the garden; although there were a great many more fruits than they could tell what to do with. The great men were so civil that notwithstanding this affront, they had no punishment upon them. But the event of this was, that a few days after, they were removed from this house to another where was a garden, but no trees in it. And because they would not allow the King a few, they lost all themselves.

I mentioned before two lads of this company, whom the King chose out for his own service. Their names were HUGH SMART and HENRY MAN. These being taken into his Court, obtained great favour and honour from him, as to be always in his presence, and very often he would kindly and familiarly talk with them, concerning their country, what it afforded, and of their King, and his strength for war.

Till at length HUGH SMART having a desire to hear news concerning England, privately got to the speech of a Dutch Ambassador. Of which the King had notice, but would not believe it, supposing the information was given him out of envy to his favourite; but commanded privately to watch him, and if he went again to catch him there: which he not being aware of, went again and was caught. At which the King was very angry: for he allows none to come to the speech of Ambassadors; much less one that served in his presence and heard and saw all that passed in Court. Yet the King dealt very favourably with him. For had it been a Cingalese, there is nothing more sure than that he should have died for it; but this Englishman's punishment was only to be sent away, and kept a prisoner in the mountains without chains: and the King ordered him to be well used there; where indeed he lived in better content than in the King's palace. He took a wife there, and had one son by her; and afterwards died by a mischance, which was thus: as he was gathering a Jak from the tree by a crook, it [? *the tree*] fell down upon his side, and bruised him; so that it killed him.

HENRY MAN, the other Englishman, yet remained in favour; and was promoted to be chief over all the King's servants that attended on him in his palace. It happened one day that he broke one of the King's china dishes: which made him so sore afraid, that he fled for sanctuary into a *vehar*, a temple where the chief priests always dwell and hold the consultations. This did not a little displease the King, this act of his supposing him to be of opinion that those priests were able to secure him against the King's displeasure. However he, showing reverence to their order, would not violently fetch him from thence; but sent a kind message to the Englishman, bidding him "not to be afraid for so small a matter as a dish"—and it is probable, had he not added this fault, he might have escaped without punishment —"and that he should come, and act in his place as formerly." At which message, he came forth; and immediately, as the King had given orders, they took hold of him, and bound his arms above the elbows behind; which is their fashion of binding men. In which manner, he lay all that night, being bound so hard that his arms swelled, and the ropes cut through the flesh into the bones. The next day the King commanded a nobleman to loose the ropes off his arms, and to put chains on his legs; and to keep him in his house, and there feed him and cure him. Thus he lay some six months, and was cured; but had no strength in his arms: and then was taken into his office again, and had as much favour from the King, as before; who seemed much to lament him for his folly, thus to procure his own ruin.

Not long after, he again offended the King; which, as it is reported, was thus. A Portuguese had been sent for to the city [of Kandy] to be employed in the King's service; to which service he had no stomach at all, and was greatly afraid thereof, as he justly might be. For the avoiding thereof, he sends a letter to this English courtier; wherein he entreated him to use his interest to excuse him to the King. The Englishman could not read the letter, it being written in the Portuguese tongue, but gave it to another to read: which when he knew the contents thereof, he thought it not safe for him to meddle in that business, and so concealed the letter. The person to whom the Englishman had given it to read, some time after informed the King thereof. Whereupon both the Portuguese that sent the letter, and the Englishman to whom it was sent, and the third person that read it (because he informed not sooner) were all three, at one time and in one place, torn in pieces by elephants.

After this execution; the King supposing that we might be either discontented in ourselves or discountenanced by the people of the land: sent special orders to all parts where we dwelt, that we should be of good cheer; and not be discouraged, neither abused by the natives.

Thus jealous is the King of letters, and allows none to come or go.

We have seen how dear it cost poor HENRY MAN. Master WILLIAM VASSAL, another of the *Persia Merchant* men, was therefore more wary of some letters he had; and came off better. This man had received several letters, as it was known abroad that he had; which he, fearing lest the King should hear of, thought it most convenient and safe to go to the Court and present them himself; that so he might plead in his own defence to the King. Which he did. He acknowledged to him that he had received letters, and that they came to his hands, a pretty while ago; but withal pretended excuses and reasons to clear himself; as that, "when he received them, he knew not that it was against the law and manner of the country; and when he did know, he took counsel of a Portuguese priest," who was now dead, "being old and, as he thought, well experienced in the country: but he advised him to defer awhile the carrying them unto the King until a more convenient season. After this, he did attempt," he said, "to bring them unto the King; but could not be permitted to have entrance through the Watches; so that until now, he could not have opportunity to present them."

The King at the hearing thereof, seemed not to be displeased in the least, but bade him read them: which he did in the English language, as they were written; and the King sat very attentive, as if he had understood every word. After they were read, the King gave VASSAL a letter he had intercepted, sent to us from Sir EDWARD WINTER, then Agent at Fort St. George [*Madras*], and asked the news and contents thereof: which Mr. VASSAL informed him of, at large. It was concerning the victory [on 3rd June 1665] we had gained over the Dutch; when OPDAM, Admiral of Holland, was slain; and concerning the number of our ships in that fight: being there specified to be an 150 sail. The King inquired much after the number of guns and men they carried. The number of men, he [Master VASSAL] computed to be, one ship with another, about 300 per ship. At which rate, the King demanded of him, how many that was in all? Which Mr. VASSAL went about to cast up in the sand, with his finger: but before he had made his figures, the King had done it by head, and bade him desist; saying it was 45,000.

This news of the Hollanders' overthrow, and the English victory much delighted the King; and he inquired into it very particularly. Then the King pretended that he would send a letter to the English nation, and bade Master VASSAL inform him of a trusty bearer: which he was very forward to do, and named one of the best of those which he had made trial of. One of the great men there present, objected against him; saying, he was insufficient, and asked him if he knew no other. At which, VASSAL suspected their design, which was to learn who had brought those letters: and so framed his answer accordingly, which was, that he knew no other.

There was much other discourse passed between the King and him at this time, in the Portuguese tongue; which, what it was, I could never get out of him, the King having commanded him to keep it secret: and he saith, he hath sworn to himself not to divulge it, till he is out of the King's hands. At parting, the King told him that for secrecy, he would send him home privately, or otherwise he would have dismissed him with drums and honour: but after this, the King never sent for him again. And the man that he named as fit and able to carry the King's letter, was sent away prisoner to be kept in chains in the country. It is supposed that they concluded him to have been the man that brought VASSAL his letters.

And thus much of the captivity and condition of the *Persia Merchant* men.

CHAPTER V.

Concerning the means that were used for our deliverance: and what happened to us in the rebellion; and how we were settled afterwards.

ALL OF us, in this manner, remained until the year 1664. At which time arrived a letter on our behalf to the King from the Right Worshipful Sir EDWARD WINTER, Governor of Fort George, and Agent there. The Dutch Ambassador also at that time, by a commission from the Governor of Colombo, treated with the King for us. With Sir EDWARD's message the King was much pleased, and with the Dutch Ambassador's mediation so prevailed with; that he promised he would send us away.

Upon this, he commanded us all to be brought to the city of Nillembe. Whither, when we came, we were very joyful, not only upon the hopes of our liberty; but also upon the sight of one another. For several of us had not seen the others, since we were first parted [in 1660]. Here also we met with the *Persia Merchant* men; whom, until this time, we had not seen. So that we were [originally] nine and twenty English in all.

Some few days after our arrival at the city, we were all called to Court. At which time, standing all of us in one of the palace courtyards, the nobles by command from the King, came forth and told us, "that it was His Majesty's pleasure to grant unto us our liberty and to send us home to our country; and that we should not any more look upon ourselves as prisoners or detained men." At which, we bowed our heads and thanked His Majesty. They told us moreover, "that the King was intending to send us either with the Dutch Ambassador or by the boat which Sir EDWARD WINTER had sent: and that it was His Majesty's goodwill to grant us our choice." We humbly referred it to His Majesty's pleasure. They answered, "His Majesty could and would do his pleasure, but his will was to know our minds." After a short consultation we answered, "Since it was his Majesty's pleasure to grant us our choice"—with many thanks and obeisance—"we chose to go with the Dutch Ambassador, fearing the boat's insufficiency." She having, as we were well sensible, laid there a great while. And if we had chosen the boat, the danger of going that way, might have served them for a put off to us; and a plea to detain us still, out of care of us: and again, had we refused the Ambassador's kindness at this time; for the future, if these things succeeded not with us now, we could never have expected any more aid or friendship from that nation. In the next place, they told us, "It was the King's pleasure to let us understand, that all those that were willing to stay and serve His Majesty; should have very great rewards, as towns, money, slaves, and places of honour conferred upon them." Which all in general refused.

Then we were bidden to absent ourselves, while they returned our answers to the King. By and bye, there came an order to call us in, one at a time, when the former promises were repeated to every one of us; of great favours, honours and rewards from the King to those that were willing to stay with him: and after each one had given his answer, he was sent into a corner of the courtyard, and then another called; and so all round, one after another: they inquiring particularly concerning each man's trade and office; handicraftsmen and trumpeters being most desired by the King. We being thus particularly examined again; there was not one of us that was tempted by the King's rewards: but all in general refused the King's honourable employment, choosing rather to go to our native country. By which we purchased the King's displeasure.

After this, they told us, that we must wait at the palace gate daily: it being the King's pleasure that we should make our personal appearance before him. In this manner, we waited many days.

At length happened a thing which he least suspected, viz., a general rebellion of his people against him; who assaulted his palace in the night, but their hearts failed them, daring not to enter the apartment where his person was. For if they had had courage enough, they might have taken him there: for he stayed in his palace until the morning, and then fled into the mountains and escaped their hands; but more through their cowardliness than his valour.

This rebellion I have related at large in the Second Part [of this book]; whither he that desires to know more of it, may have recourse. Only I shall mention here a few things concerning ourselves, who were gotten [*had got*] into the midst of these broils and combustions; being all of us now waiting upon the King in the city of Nillembe.

We here break off Captain KNOX's narrative, to give his account of this rising, from the Second Part referred to.

A relation of the rebellion made against the King.

IT HAPPENED in the year 1664 A.D. About which time appeared a fearful blazing star [*a comet*]. Just at the instant of the rebellion, the star was right over our heads. And one thing I very much wondered at was, that whereas before this rebellion, the tail stood away towards the westward; from which side the rebellion sprang: the very night after—for I well observed it—the tail turned, and stood away toward the eastward; and by degrees it diminished quite away.

At this time, I say, the people of this land, having been long and sore oppressed by this King's unreasonable and cruel government, had contrived a plot against him: which was to assault the King's Court in the night, and slay him; and to make the Prince his son, king—he being then some twelve or fifteen years of age—who was then with his mother the Queen in the city of Kandy.

At this time the King held his Court in a city called Nillembe: the situation of which is far inferior to that of Kandy; and as far beyond that of Digligy where he now is. Nillembe lieth some fourteen miles southward of the city of Kandy. In the place where this city stands, it is reported by tradition that an hare gave chase after a dog; upon which it was concluded that that place was fortunate: and so indeed it proved to the King. It is environed with hills and woods.

The time appointed to put their design in action was the 21st of December 1664, about twelve in the night. Having got a select company of men—how many I know not well, but as it is supposed not above 200; neither needed they many here, having so many confederates in the Court—in the dead of the night, they came marching into the city.

The Watch was thought to be of their confederacy: but if he were not; it was not in his power to resist them. Howbeit afterwards, whether he were or not, he was executed for it.

The said men being thus in the city, hastened and came down to the Court; and fell upon the great men [*nobles*] which then lay without the palace upon watch—since which time, by the King's order, they lie always within the palace—for they were well informed beforehand, who were for them and who not. Many who before were not intrusted to know of their design, were killed and wounded: and those that could, seeing the slaughter of others, got in unto the King; who was walled about with a clay wall, thatched. That was all his strength. Yet these people feared to assault him; lying still until the morning.

At which time, the King made way to flee—fearing to stay in his palace—endeavouring to get unto the mountains. He had not with him above fifty persons. There went with him horses; but the ways were so bad, that he could not ride: they were fain to drive an elephant before him, to break the way through the woods; that the King with his followers might pass.

As he fled, they pursued him; but at a great distance, fearing to approach within shot of him: for he wanted not excellent fowling pieces; which are made there. So he got safe upon a mountain called Gauluda, some fifteen miles distant; where many of the inhabitants that were near, resorted to him. Howbeit had the people of the rebel party been resolute—who were the major part and almost of all the land—this hill could not have secured him, but they might have driven him from thence; there being many ways by which they might have ascended.

There is not far from thence, a high and peaked hill called Mondamounour; where there is but one way to get up, and that very steep: at the top are great stones hanging in chains to let fall when need requireth. Had he fled thither, there had been no way to come at him: but he never will adventure to go, where he may be stopped in.

The people having thus driven away the old King, marched away to the city of Kandy, and proclaimed the Prince, king; giving out to us English who were there, that what they had done they had not done rashly, but upon good consideration and with good advice: the King by his evil government having occasioned it; who went about to destroy them and their country—as in keeping Ambassadors, disannulling of trade, detaining all people that came upon his land, killing his subjects and their children, and not suffering them to enjoy nor to see their wives. All this was contrary to reason; and as they were informed, to the government of other countries

The Prince being young and tender, and having never been out of the palace, nor ever seen any but those that attended on his person; was—as it seemed afterwards—scared to see so many coming and bowing down to him, and telling him that he was King; and that his father was fled into the mountains. Neither did he say or act anything; as not owning the business or else not knowing what to say or do. This much discouraged the rebels, to see they had no more thanks for their pains. And so all things stood until the 25th of December, at which time they intended to march and fall upon the old King.

But in the interim, the King's sister flies away with the Prince from the Court into the country near unto the King: which so amazed the rebels, that they scattered about the money, cloth and plunder which they had taken, and were going to distribute to the strangers to gain their goodwill and assistance; and fled. Others of their company seeing the business was overthrown; to make amends for their former fact, turned and fell on their consorts [*confederates*], killing and taking prisoners all they could. The people were now all up in arms one against another: killing whom they pleased, only saying they were rebels; and taking their goods.

By this time, a great man [*nobleman*] had drawn out his men, and stood in the field: and there turned, and publicly declared for the old King; and so went to catch the rebels that were scattered abroad: who—when he understood that they were all fled, and no whole party or body left to resist him—marched into the city killing all he could catch.

And so all revolted, and came back to the King again: whilst he only lay still upon his mountain. The King needed not to take care to catch or execute the rebels, for they themselves out of their zeal to him and to make amends for what was past; imprisoned and killed all they met, the plunder being their own. This continued for eight or ten days.

Which the King hearing of, commanded to kill no more: but that whom they took, they should imprison until examination was passed: which was not so much to save innocent persons from violence as that he might have the rebels; to torment them and make them confess their confederates. For he spared none that appeared guilty. Some to this day lie chained in prison; being sequestered from all their estates, and beg for their living.

One of the most notable rebels, called AMBOM WELLARAUL; he sent to Colombo to the Dutch to execute; supposing they would invent new tortures for him, beyond what he knew of: but they—instead of executing him—cut off his chains, and entertained him kindly; and there he is still in the city of Colombo, they reserving him for some designs they may hereafter have against that country.

The King could not but be sensible but that it was his rigorous government that had occasioned this rebellion: yet he amended it not in the least; but on the contrary, like to REHOBOAM, added yet more to the people's yoke.

And being thus safely reinstated in his kingdom again: and observing that the life of his son gave encouragement to the rebellion; he resolved to prevent it for the future by taking him away: which upon the next opportunity he did by poisoning him [pretending to send physic to cure him, when he was sick].

But one thing there is, that argues him guilty of imprudence and horrible ingratitude: that most of those that went along with him when he fled, of whose loyalty he had such ample experience, he has since cut off; and that with extreme cruelty too.

In the month of February, 1666; there appeared in this country another comet or stream in the west; the head end under the horizon, much resembling that which was seen in England in December, 1680. The sight of this did much daunt both King and people: having but a year or two before felt the sad event of a blazing star in this rebellion which I have now related. The King sent men upon the highest mountains in the land to look if they could perceive the head of it: which they could not, it being still under the horizon. This continued visible about the space of one month: and by that time it was so diminished that it could not be seen.

But there were no remarkable passages that ensued upon it.

We now resume our Author's narration.

It was a great and marvellous mercy of Almighty GOD to bring us safe through these dangers; for it so happened all along, that we were in the very midst of them. Before they gave the assault on the King's palace; they were consulting to lay hands on us: fearing lest we might be prejudicial to their business in joining to the help and assistance of the King against them. For though we were but few in comparison; yet the name of white men was somewhat dreadful to them: whereupon, at first, their counsels were to cut us off. But others among them advised, that it would be better to let us alone, "for that we, being ignorant of their designs"—as indeed we were—"and quiet in our several lodgings; could not be provided to hurt or endanger them: but otherwise, if they should lay hands on us, it would certainly come to the King's ears, and alarm him; and then all would be frustrated and overthrown." This, some of their own party have related to us since. These counsels were not given out of any secret goodwill any of them bore to us, as I believe: but proceeded from the overruling hand of GOD, who put those things into their hearts for our safety and preservation.

The people of the city of Nillembe, whence the King fled, ran away also; leaving their houses and goods behind them: where we found good prey and plunder, being permitted to ransack the houses of all such as were fled away with the King.

The rebels having driven away the King, and marching to the city of Kandy to the Prince, carried us along with them; the chief of their party telling us that we should now be of good cheer, for what they had done they had done upon very good advisement; the King's ill-government having given an occasion to it: who went about to destroy them and their country: and particularly insisted upon such things as might be plausible to strangers, such as keeping the Ambassadors, discouraging trade, detaining of foreigners that came upon his land, besides his cruelties towards themselves that were his natural people. All which, they told us, they had been informed was contrary to the government of other countries; and now so soon as their business was settled, they assured us, they would detain none that were minded to go to their own country.

Being now at Kandy, on Christmas Day, of all the days in the year; they sent to call us to the Court, and gave us some money and clothes first, to make us the more willing to take up arms; which they intended then to deliver unto us, and to go with them upon a design to fall upon the old King in the palace whither he was fled. But in the very interim of time, GOD being merciful unto us; the Prince with his aunt fled: which so amazed and discouraged them, that the money and clothes which they were distributing to us and other strangers, to gain us over to them, they scattered about the courtyard; and fled themselves. And now followed nothing but the cutting of one another's throats, to make themselves appear the more loyal subjects and make amends for their former rebellion.

We, for our parts, little thinking in what danger we were, fell into a scramble among the rest, to get what we could of the money that was strewed about; being then in great necessity and want. For the allowance which formerly we had, was in this disturbance lost; and so we remained without it for some three months; the want of which, this money did help to supply.

Having gotten what we could at the Court, we made our way to get out of the hurly-burly, to our lodgings: intending, as we were strangers and prisoners neither to meddle nor to make on the one side or the other; being well satisfied, if GOD would but permit us quietly to sit and eat such a Christmas dinner together, as He had prepared for us.

For our parts, we had no other dealings with the rebels, than to desire them to permit us to go to our native country; which liberty they promised we should not want long. But being sent for by them to the Court, we durst not but go;

and they giving us such things as we wanted, we could not refuse to take them. But the day being turned, put us into great fear; doubting how the King would take it at our hands, from whom, we knew, this could not be hid.

Into our houses, we got safely: but no sooner were we there; but immediately we were called again by a great man, who had drawn out his men, and stood in the field. This man, we thought, had been one of the rebels who to secure himself upon this change, had intended to run away down to Colombo to the Dutch; which made us repair to him the more cheerfully, leaving our meat a roasting on the spit: but it proved otherwise. For no sooner had he gotten us unto him, but he proclaimed himself for the old King; and forthwith he and his company, taking us with him, marched away to fight or seize the rebels; but meeting none, went into the city of Kandy and there dismissed us, saying, "he would acquaint the King how willing and ready we were to fight for him, if need had required." Although, GOD knows, it was the least of our thoughts and intents: yet GOD brought it to pass for our good. For when the King was informed of what we had received of the rebels: this piece of good service that we had done or rather were supposed to have done, was also told him. At the hearing of which, he himself justified us to be innocent, saying, "Since my absence, who was there that would give them victuals?" and, "It was mere want that made them to take what they did." Thus the words of the King's own mouth acquitted us: and when the sword devoured on every side; yet by the Providence of GOD, not one hair of our heads perished.

The tumults being appeased and the rebellion vanquished; the king was settled in his throne again. And all this happened in five days.

We were now greatly necessitated for food, and wanted some fresh orders from the King's mouth for our future subsistence. So that having no other remedy, we were fain to go and lay in the highway that leads to the city of Kandy a begging: for the people would not let us go any nearer towards the King, as we would have done. There therefore we lay, that the King might come to a knowledge of us; and give command for our allowance again. By which means, we obtained our purpose. For having lain there some two months, the King was pleased to appoint our quarters in the country as formerly; not mentioning a word of sending us away, as he had made us believe before the rebellion.

Now we were all sent away indeed, not into our own country districts, but into new quarters: which being such as GOD would have to be no better, we were glad it was so well; being sore a weary of lying in this manner. We were all now placed one in a town, as formerly; together with the *Persia Merchant* men also, who hitherto had lived in the city of Kandy, and had their provisions brought them out of the King's palace ready dressed. These were now sent away with us into the country: and as strict charge was given for our good entertainment, as before.

We were thus dispersed about the towns, here one and there another, for the more convenient receiving of our allowance, and for the greater ease of the people. And now we were far better to pass [*in a far better pass*] than heretofore; having the language and being acquainted with the manners and customs of the people; and we had the same proportion of victuals and the like respect as formerly.

And now they fell into employments as they pleased, either husbandry or merchandizing or knitting caps; being altogether free to do what they will themselves, and to go where they will, except running away: and for that end, we were not permitted to go down to the sea; but we might travel all about the country, and no man regarded us. For though the people, some of the first years of our captivity, would scarcely let us go any whither, and had an eye upon us afterwards; yet in process of time, all their suspicions of our going away wore off: especially when several of the English had built them houses; and others had taken them wives, by whom they had children, to the number of eighteen living, when I came away.

Having said all this in general of the English people there, I will now continue a further account of myself.

CHAPTER VI.

A continuation of the Author's particular condition after rebellion. He purchaseth a piece of land.

MY HAP was to be quartered in a country called Handapondoun, lying to the westward of the city of Kandy; which place liked [*pleased*] me very well, being much nearer to the sea than where I dwelt before; which gave me some probable hopes, that in time I might chance to make an escape. But in the mean time, to free myself from the suspicion of the people—who watched me by night, and by day had an eye to all my actions—I went to work, with the help of some of my neighbours to build me another house, upon the bank of a river; and intrenched it round with a ditch, and planted an hedge: and so began to settle myself, and followed my business of knitting, and going about the country a trading; seeming to be very well contented in this condition.

Lying so long at the city [of Kandy] without allowance, I had spent all to some seven shillings; which served me for a stock to set up again in these new quarters: and—by the blessing of my most gracious GOD, which never failed me in all my undertakings—I soon came to be well furnished with what that country afforded. Insomuch that my neighbours and townsmen no more suspected my running away; but earnestly advised me to marry, saying "it would be an ease and help to me:" knowing that I then dressed my victuals myself; having turned my boy to seek his fortune, when we were at the city of Kandy. They urged also, "that it was not convenient for a young man as I was to live so solitarily alone in a house; and if it should so come to pass that the King should send me hereafter to my country, their manner of marriage," they said, "was not like ours, and I might without any offence, discharge my wife, and go away."

I seemed not altogether to slight their counsel, that they might the less suspect that I had any thoughts of mine own country; but told them, that, "as yet, I was not sufficiently stocked," and also, "that I would look for one that I could love," though in my heart I never purposed any such matter; but on the contrary, did heartily abhor all thoughts tending that way.

In this place I lived two years and all that time, could not get one likely occasion of running for it; for I thought it better to forbear running too great a hazard, by being over hasty to escape; than to deprive myself of all hopes for the future, when time and experience would be a great help to me.

In the year 1666, the Hollanders came up and built a fort just below me; there being but a ridge of mountains between them and me; but though so near, I could not come to them, a Watch being kept at every passage. The King sent down against them two great commanders with their armies; but being not strong enough to expel them; they lay in these Watches to stop them from coming up higher. The name of this fort was called Arranderre: which although they could not prevent the Dutch from building at that time; yet some years after, when they were not aware, they fell upon it and took it; and brought all the people of it up to Kandy, where those that remained alive were, when I came from thence.

In this country [*county*] of Hotterakorle where the Dutch had built this fort; were four Englishmen placed, whereof I was one. Respecting all of whom, the King immediately upon the news of the Dutch invasion, sent orders to bring up out of the danger of the war into Conde Uda; fearing that which we were intending to do, viz.—to run away.

This invasion happening so unexpectedly, and our remove being so sudden: I was forced to leave behind me that little estate which GOD had given me, being scattered abroad in betel nuts, the great commodity of that country; which I was then in parting from. Much ado I had to get my clothes brought along with me; the enemies, as they called them (but my friends) being so near. And thus I was carried out of this county as poor as I came into it, leaving all the fruits of my labour and industry behind me: which called to my remembrance the words of JOB, "Naked came I into this world, and naked shall I return. GOD gave and GOD hath taken away. Blessed be the name of the LORD."

We all four were brought together up into a town on the top of a mountain, called Lagoondenia: where I and my dear friend and fellow-prisoner Master JOHN LOVELAND, lived together in one house. For by this time, not many of our people were as we were, that is, single men: but seeing so little hope, despaired of their liberty; and had taken wives or bedfellows.

At our first coming into this town, we were very much dismayed: it being one of the most dismal places that I have seen upon that land. It stands alone upon the top of a mountain and no other town near it, and has not above four or five houses in it. And oftentimes into this town, did the King use to send such malefactors as he was minded suddenly to cut off. Upon these accounts, our being brought to this place, could not but scare us; and the more because it was the King's special order and command to place us in this very town.

But this our trouble and dejection, thanks be to GOD! lasted but a day; for the King seemed to apprehend into what a fit of fear and sorrow, this our remove would cast us; and to be sensible, how sadly we must needs take it to change a sweet and pleasant country such as Handapondoun and the country adjacent was, for this most sad and dismal mountain. And therefore the next day came a comfortable message from the King's own mouth, sent by no less a man than he who had the chief power and command over those people, who were appointed to give us our victuals, where we were. This message which, as he said himself, he was ordered by the King to deliver to the people in our hearing, was this, "That they should not think that we were malefactors, that is, such, who having incurred the King's displeasure, were sent to be kept prisoners there; but men whom his Majesty did highly esteem and meant to promote to great honour in his service; and that they should respect us as such, and entertain us accordingly. And if their ability would not reach thereunto, it was the King's order," he said, "to bid them sell their cattle and goods, and when that was done, their wives and children: rather than we should want of our due allowance," which he ordered should be as formerly we used to have: "and if we had not houses thatched and sufficient for us to dwell in," he said, "we should change and take theirs."

This kind order from the King coming so suddenly, did not a little comfort and encourage us: for then we did perceive the King's purpose and intent in placing us in those remote parts, was not to punish us, but there that we might be his instruments to plague and take revenge of that people; who it seems had plundered the King's palace in the time of the late rebellion, when he left it and fled, for this town lies near unto the same [i.e. *Nillembe*]. And their office lying about the Court, they had the fairer opportunity of plundering it: for the service they have to perform to the King is to carry his palanquin, when he pleaseth to ride therein; and also to bring milk every morning to the Court, they being keepers of the King's cattle.

In this town we remained some three years, by which time we were grown quite weary of the place; and the place and people also grown weary of us, who were but troublesome guests to them; for having such great authority given us over them, we would not lose it; and being four of us in call one of another, we would not permit or suffer them to domineer over us. Being thus tired with one another's company, and the King's order being of an old date, we used all the means we could to clear ourselves of one another; often repairing unto the Court to seek to obtain a license that we might be removed and placed anywhere else; but there was none that durst grant it, because it was the King's peculiar command and special appointment that we must abide in that very town.

During the time of our stay here, we had our victuals brought us in good order and due season, the inhabitants having such a charge given them by their Governor, and he from the King; durst not do otherwise: so that we had but little to do; only to dress and eat, and sit down to knit.

I had used the utmost of my skill and endeavour to get a license to go down to my former quarters, all things being now pretty well settled; hoping that I might recover some of my old debts: but by no means could I obtain it. The denial of so reasonable a desire, put me upon taking leave. I was well acquainted with the way, but yet I hired a man to go with me; without which I could not get through the Watches: for although I was the master and he the man; yet when we came into the Watches; he was the keeper and I the prisoner. And by this means we passed without being suspected.

Being come into my old quarters, by pretending that this man was sent down from the magistrate to see that my debts and demands might be duly paid and discharged, I chanced to recover some of them; and the rest I gave over for lost: for I never more looked after them. And so I began the world anew; and, by the blessing of GOD, was again pretty well recruited, before I left this town.

In the time of my residence here [at Lagoondenia], I chanced to hear of a small piece of land that was to be sold; about which I made very diligent inquiry: for although I was sore a weary of living in this town, yet I could not get out of it; not having other new quarters appointed me, unless I could provide a place for myself to remove to; which now GOD had put into my hand. As for the King's command I dreaded it not much, having found by observation that the King's orders wore away by time, and that the neglect of them comes at last to be unregarded. However I was resolved to put it to the hazard, come what would.

Although I had been now some seven or eight years in this land, and by this time came to know pretty well the customs and constitutions of the nation, yet I would not trust my own knowledge; but to prevent the worst, I went to the Governor of that same country where the land lay, to desire his advice, whether or not I might lawfully buy that small piece of land. He inquired "whose, and what land it was?" I informed him "that it had been formerly dedicated to a priest, and he at his death had left it to his grandson; who for want, was forced to sell it." Understanding this, the Governor approved of the business, and encouraged me to buy it; saying "that such kind of lands only, were lawful here to be bought and sold, and that this was not in the least litigious."

Having gotten both his consent and advice, I went on cheerfully with my purchase. The place also liked [*pleased*] me wondrously well: it being a point of land, standing into a cornfield; so that cornfields were on three sides of it, and just before my door, a little corn ground belonging thereto and very well watered. In the ground besides eight cocoa-nut trees, there were all sorts of fruit trees that the country afforded. But it had been so long desolate that it was all overgrown with bushes, and had no sign of a house therein.

The price of this land was five and twenty larees, that is, five dollars, a great sum of money in the account of this country: yet—thanks be to GOD! who had so far enabled me after my late and great loss—I was strong enough to lay this down. The terms of purchase being concluded on between us, a writing was made upon a leaf after that country's manner, witnessed by seven or eight men of the best quality in the town, which was delivered to me; and I paid the money, and then took possession of the land. It lies some ten miles to the southward of the city of Kandy in the county of Oodanowera, in the town of Elledat.

Now I went about building a house upon my land, and was assisted by three of my countrymen that dwelt near by; ROGER GOLD, RALPH KNIGHT, and STEPHEN RUTLAND: and in a short time, we finished it. The country people were all well pleased to see us thus busy ourselves about buying of land, and building of houses; thinking it would tie our minds the faster to their country, and make us think the less upon our own.

Though I had built my new house, yet durst I not yet leave my old quarters in Lagoondenia, but waited until a more convenient time fell out for that purpose. I went away therefore to my old home; and left my aforesaid three English neighbours to inhabit it in my absence.

Not long after, I found a fit season to be gone to my estate at Elledat: and upon my going the rest [of the four] left the town [of Lagoondenia] also, and went and dwelt elsewhere; each one lived where he best liked. But by this means, we all lost a privilege which we had before; which was, that our victuals were brought unto us: and now we were forced to go and fetch them ourselves; the people alleging, truly enough, that they were not bound to carry our provisions about the country after us.

Being settled in my new house, I began to plant ground full of all sorts of fruit trees, which, by the blessing of GOD, all grew and prospered, and yielded me plenty and good increase; sufficient both for me and those that dwelt with me: for the three Englishmen I left at my house when I departed back to Lagoondenia, still lived with me.

We were all single men, and we agreed very well together,

and were helpful to one another. And for their help and assistance, I freely granted them liberty to use and enjoy whatsoever the ground afforded, as much as myself. And, with a joint consent, it was concluded amongst us, "that only single men and bachelors should dwell there; and that such as would not be conformable to this present agreement, should depart and absent himself from our society; and also forfeit his right and claim to the forementioned privilege, that is, to be cut off from all benefit of whatsoever the trees and ground afforded."

I thought fit to make such a covenant, to exclude women from coming in among us, to prevent all strife and dissension, and to make all possible provision for the keeping up of love and quietness among ourselves.

In this manner, we four lived together some two years very lovingly and contentedly; not an ill word passing between us. We used to take turns in keeping at home, while the rest went forth about their business. For our house stood alone, and had no neighbour near it: therefore we always left one within. The rest of the Englishmen lived round about us; some four or five miles distant, and some more: so that we were, as it were, within reach one of another, which made us like our present situation the more.

Thus we lived upon the mountains, being beset round about us with Watches, most of our people being now married: so that now all talk and suspicion of our running away was laid aside; neither indeed was it scarcely possible. The effect of which was that now we could walk from one to the other, or where we would upon the mountains; no man molesting or disturbing us in the least: so that we began to go about a pedling and trading in the country further towards the northward, carrying our caps about to sell.

By this time, two of our company [ROGER GOLD and RALPH KNIGHT] seeing but little hopes of liberty, thought it too hard a task thus to lead a single life; and married: which when they had done, according to the former agreement, they departed from us.

So that our company was now reduced to two, namely, myself and STEPHEN RUTLAND; whose inclination and resolution was as steadfast as mine against marriage. And we parted not to the last, but came away together.

CHAPTER VII.

A return to the rest of the English, with some further accounts of them. And some further discourse of the Author's course of life.

LET us now make a visit to the rest of our countrymen; and see how they do.

They reckoning themselves in for their lives, in order to their future settlement, were generally disposed to marry; concerning which we have had many and sundry disputes among ourselves: as particularly, concerning the lawfulness of matching with heathens and idolaters, and whether the Cingalese marriage were any better than living in whoredom, there being no Christian priests to join them together; and it being allowed by their laws, to change their wives and take others, as often as they pleased.

But these cases we solved for our own advantage, after this manner, "that we were but flesh and blood;" and that it is said "it is better to marry than to burn;" and that, "as far as we could see, we were cut off from all marriages anywhere else, even for our lifetime, and therefore that we must marry with these or with none at all: and when the people in Scripture were forbidden to take wives of strangers, it was then when they might intermarry with their own people, and so no necessity lay on them; and that when they could not, there are examples in the Old Testament upon record, that they took wives of the daughters of the land, wherein they dwelt."

These reasons being urged, there were none among us, that could object ought against them: especially if those that were minded to marry women here did take them for their wives during their lives; as some of them say they do, and most of the women they marry are such as do profess themselves to be Christians.

As for mine own part, however lawful these marriages might be, yet I judged it far more convenient for me to abstain, and that it more redounded to my good, having always a reviving hope in me that my GOD had not forsaken me, but that according to his gracious promise to the Jews in the 30th chapter of Deuteronomy, and the beginning, "would turn my captivity, and bring me into the land of my fathers." These and such like meditations, together with my prayers to GOD, kept me from that unequal yoke of unbelievers; which several of my countrymen and fellow-prisoners put themselves under.

By this time, our people, having plied their business hard, had almost knit themselves out of work; and now caps were become a very dead commodity, which were the chief stay they had heretofore to trust to. So that now, most of them betook themselves to other employments: some to husbandry, ploughing ground, and sowing rice and keeping cattle; others distilled arrack to sell: others went about the country a trading. For that which one part of the land affords is a good commodity to carry to another that wants it. And thus, with the help of a little allowance, they make a shift to subsist. Most of their wives spin cotton yarn; which is a great help to them for clothing; and, at spare times, also knit.

After this manner, by the blessing of GOD, our nation hath lived and still doth, in as good a fashion as any other people or nation whatsoever that are strangers there, or as any of the natives themselves: the grandees and courtiers only excepted. This I speak to the praise and glory of our GOD, who loves the stranger in giving him food and raiment; and that hath been pleased to give us favour and a good repute in the sight of our enemies. We cannot complain for want of justice in any wrongs we have sustained by the people, or that our cause hath been discountenanced: but rather that we have been favoured above the natives themselves.

One of our men happened to be beaten by a neighbour. At which, we were very much concerned, taking it as a reproach to our nation; and fearing that it might embolden others to do the like by the rest of us: therefore, with joint consent, we all concluded to go to the Court to complain, and to desire satisfaction from the Adigar. Which we did. Upon this, the man who had beaten the Englishman was summoned in, to appear before him: who, seeing so many of us there and fearing the cause would go very hard with him, to make the judge his friend, gave him a bribe. He having received it, would have shifted off the punishment from the malefactor: but we, day after day, followed him from house to Court and from place to place, wherever he went; demanding justice and satisfaction for the wrong we had received, and showing the black and blue blows upon the Englishman's shoulders to all the rest of the noblemen at Court. He, fearing therefore lest the King might be made acquainted therewith, was forced —though much against his will—to clap the Cingalese in chains. In which condition, after he had got him; he released him not, till besides the former fee, he had given him another.

Lately [*i.e.* about 1678], was RICHARD VARNHAM taken into the King's service, and held as honourable employment as ever any Christian had, in my time; being Commander of 970 soldiers, and set over all the great guns; and besides this several towns were put under him. A place of no less profit than honour. The King gave him an excellent silver sword and halbert, the like to which the King never gave to any white man in my time. But he had the good luck to die a natural death: for had not that prevented, in all probability he should have followed the two Englishmen spoken of before, that served him.

Some years since, some of our nation took up arms under the King: which happened on this occasion. The Hollanders had a small fort in the King's country, called Bibligom fort. This the King minding to take and demolish, sent his army to besiege it; but it was pretty strong: for there were about ninety Dutchmen in it besides a good number of black soldiers; and it had four guns, on each point of the compass one. Being in this condition, it held out.

Some of the great men informed the King of several Dutch runaways in his land that might be trusted, as not daring to turn again, for fear of the gallows; who might help to reduce the fort: and that also there were white men of other nations that had wives and children from whom they would not run; and that these might do him good service. Unto this advice the King inclined. Whereupon the King made a declaration to invite the foreign nations into his service against

Bibligom fort, that he would compel none, but that such as were willing of their own free accord, the King would take it kindly, and they should be well rewarded.

Now there entered into the King's service upon this expedition, some of all nations; both Portuguese, Dutch, and English; about the number of thirty. To all that took arms, he gave the value of twenty shillings in money, and three pieces of calico for clothes: and commanded them to wear breeches, hats, and doublets; a great honour there. The King intended a Dutchman, who had been an old servant to him, to be captain over them all: but the Portuguese not caring to be under the command of a Dutchman, desired a captain of their own nation; which the King granted, studying to please them at this time. But the English, being but six, were too few to have a captain over them; and so were forced some to serve under the Dutch, and some under the Portuguese captain. There were no more of the English, because being left at their liberty, they thought it safest to dwell at home; and cared not much to take arms under a heathen against Christians.

They were all ready to go, their arms and amunition ready, with guns prepared to send down; but before they went, tidings came that the fort yielded at the King's mercy. After this, the whites thought they had got an advantage of the King, in having these gifts for nothing: but the King did not intend to part with them so, but kept them to watch at his gate; and now they are reduced to great poverty and necessity.

For since the King's first gift, they have never received any pay or allowance: though they have often made their addresses to him to supply their wants; signifying their forwardness to serve him faithfully. He speaks them fair, and tells them he will consider them; but does not in the least regard them. Many of them since, after three or four years' service, have been glad to get other poor runaway Dutchmen to serve in their steads; giving them as much money and clothes as they received from the King before, that so they might get free to come home to their wives and children.

The Dutch captain would afterwards have forced the rest of the English to have come under him, and called them "traitors," because they would not; and threatened them: but they scorned him and bid him do his worst, and would never be persuaded to be soldiers under him; saying, that "it was not so much his zeal to the King's service, as his own pride to make himself greater, by having more men under him."

I will now turn to the progress of my own story.

It was now about the year 1672. I related before, that my family was reduced to two, myself and one honest man more. We lived solitarily and contented, being well settled in a good house of my own. Now we fell to breeding up goats. We begun with two, but, by the blessing of GOD, they soon came to a good many; and their flesh served us instead of mutton. We kept hens and hogs also. And seeing no sudden likelihood of liberty, we went about to make all things handsome and convenient about us; which might be serviceable to us while we lived there, and might further our liberty, whensoever we should see an occasion to attempt it: which it did, in taking away all suspicion from the people concerning us; who—not having wives as the others had—they might well think, lay the readier to take any advantage to make an escape. Which indeed we two did plot and consult about between ourselves, with all imaginable privacy, long before we could go away: and therefore we laboured, by all means, to hide our designs, and to free them from so much as suspicion.

We had now brought our house and ground to such a perfection, that few noblemen's seats in the land could excel us. On each side was a great thorn gate for entrance, which is the manner of that country. The gates of the city are of the same. We built also another house in the yard, all open for air; for ourselves to sit in, or any neighbours that came to talk with us. For seldom should we be alone; our neighbours oftener frequenting our house than we desired: out of whom to be sure, we could pick no profit; for their coming was always either to beg or to borrow. For although we were strangers and prisoners in their land, yet they would confess that Almighty GOD had dealt far more bountifully with us than with them, in that we had a far greater plenty of all things than they.

I now began to set up a new trade. For the trade of knitting was grown dead: and husbandry I could not follow, not having a wife to help and assist me therein; a great part of husbandry properly belonging to the woman to manage. Whereupon I perceived a trade in use among them, which was to lend out corn: the benefit of which was fifty per cent. per annum. This I saw to be the easiest and most profitable way of living: whereupon I took in hand to follow it; and what stock I had, I converted into corn or rice in the husk. And now as customers came for corn, I let them have it; to receive back at their next harvest, when their own corn was ripe, the same quantity I had lent them, and half as much more. But as the profit is great, so is the trouble of getting it in also. For he that useth this trade must watch when the debtor's field is ripe and claim his due in time; otherwise other creditors coming before him, will seize all upon the account of their debts, and leave no corn at all for those that come later. For these that come thus a borrowing, generally carry none of their corn home when it is ripe: for their creditors ease them of that labour, by coming into their fields and taking it; and commonly they have not half enough to pay what they owe. So that they that miss getting their debts this year, must stay till the next; when it will be doubled, two measures for one; but the interest never runs up higher, though the debt lies seven years unpaid. By means thereof I was put to a great deal of trouble; and was forced to watch early and late to get in my debts, and many times missed of them after all my pains. Howbeit when my stock did increase so that I had dealings with many; it mattered not if I lost in some places; the profit of the rest was sufficient to bear that out.

And thus, by the blessing of GOD, my little was increased to a great deal. For He had blessed me so, that I was able to lend to my enemies; and had no need to borrow of them: so that I might use the words of JACOB, not out of pride of myself, but thankfulness to GOD, "that He brought me hither with my staff, and blessed me so here, that I became two bands."

For some years together after I had removed to my own house from Lagoondenia, the people from whence I came continued my allowance, that I had when I lived among them; but now in plain terms, they told me "they could give it to me no more; and that I was better able to live without it, than they to give it me:" which though I knew to be true, yet I thought not fit to lose that portion of allowance, which the King was pleased to allow me. Therefore I went to Court and appealed to the Adigar, to whom such matters did belong: who upon consideration of the people's poor condition, appointed me monthly to come to him at the King's palace for a ticket to receive my allowance out of the King's storehouses.

Hereby I was brought into a great danger; out of which I had much ado to escape, and that with the loss of my allowance for ever after. I shall relate the manner of it in the next chapter.

CHAPTER VIII

How the Author had like to have been received into the King's service, and what means he used to avoid it. He meditates and attempts an escape; but is often prevented.

THIS frequent appearance at the Court, and waiting there for my tickets; brought me to be taken notice of by the great men, insomuch "that they wondered I had been all this while forgotten, and never been brought before the King; being so fit, as they would suppose me, for his use and service;" saying, "that from henceforward I should fare better than that allowance amounted to; as soon as the King was made acquainted with me." Which words of theirs served instead of a ticket. Whereupon fearing that I should suddenly be brought in to the King, which thing I most of all feared and least desired; and hoping that out of sight might prove out of mind, I resolved to forsake the Court, and never more to ask for tickets: especially seeing GOD had dealt so bountifully with me as to give me ability to live well enough without them: as when Israel had eaten of the corn of the land of Canaan, the manna ceased; so when I was driven to forego my allowance that had all this while sustained me in this wilderness, GOD in other ways provided for me.

From this time forward to the time of my flight out of the land, which was five years; I neither had nor demanded any more allowance: and glad I was that I could escape so.

But I must have more trouble first. For, some four or five days after my last coming from Court, there came a soldier to me, sent from the Adigar, with an order in writing under his hand, "that upon sight thereof, I should immediately dispatch and come to the Court, to make my personal appearance before the King: and that in case of any delay, the officers of the country were thereby authorized and commanded to assist the bearer, and to see the same order speedily performed."

The chief occasion of this, had been a person, not long before my near neighbour and acquaintance, OWA MATTERAL by name, who knew my manner of life, and had often been at my house; but now was taken in and employed at Court: and he out of friendship and goodwill to me, was one of the chief actors in this business, that he might bring me to preferment at Court.

Upon the abovesaid summons, there was no remedy, but to Court I must go. Where I first applied myself to my said old neighbour, OWA MATTERAL, who was the occasion of sending for me. I signified to him "that I was come in obedience to the warrant; and I desired to know the reason why I was sent for." To which he answered, "Here is good news for you. Your are to appear in the King's presence, where you will find great favour and honourable entertainment; far more than any of your countrymen yet have found." Which the great man thought would be a strong inducement to persuade me joyfully to accept of the King's employments. But this was the thing I always most dreaded, and endeavoured to shun; knowing that being taken into Court would be a means to cut off all hopes of liberty from me; which was the thing that I esteemed as equal unto life itself.

Seeing myself brought into this pass, wherein I had no earthly helper, I recommended my cause to GOD; desiring Him in whose hands are the hearts of kings and princes, to divert the business: and my cause being just and right, I was resolved to persist in a denial. My case seemed to me to be like that of the four lepers at the gate of Samaria. No avoiding of death for me. If out of ambition and honour, I should have embraced the King's service; besides the depriving myself of all hopes of liberty, in the end I must be put to death, as happens to all that serve him: and to deny his service, could be but death; and it seemed to me, to be the better death of the two. For if I should be put to death, only because I refused his service; I should be pitied as one that died innocently: but if I should be executed in his service, however innocent I was, I should be certainly reckoned a rebel and a traitor; as they all are, whom he commands to be cut off.

Upon these considerations, having thus set my resolutions, as GOD enabled me, I returned him this answer. "First, that the English nation to whom I belonged, had never done any violence or wrong to their King, either in word or deed. Secondly, that the causes of my coming on their land was not like that of other nations, who were either enemies taken in war; or such as by reason of poverty or distress, were driven to sue for relief, out of the King's bountiful liberality; or such as fled for the fear of deserved punishment: whereas, as they all well knew, I came not upon any of these causes, but on account of trade; and came ashore to receive the King's orders, which by notice we understood were come concerning us, and to render an account to the Dissauva of the reasons and occasions of our coming into the King's port. And that by the grief and sorrow I had undergone, by being so long detained from my native country—but, for which I thanked the King's majesty, without want of anything—I scarcely enjoyed myself: for my heart was always absent from my body." Hereunto adding, my insufficiency and inability for such honourable employment; being subject to many infirmities and diseases of body.

To this he replied, "Cannot you read and write English? servile labour the King requireth not of you."

I answered, "When I came ashore I was but young, and that which I then knew, now I had forgotten for want of practice; having had neither ink nor paper ever since I came ashore." I urged moreover "that it was contrary to the custom and practice of all kings and princes upon the earth, to keep and detain men that came into their countries upon such peaceable accounts as we did; much less to compel them to serve them, beyond their power and ability."

At my first coming before him, he looked very pleasingly, and spake with a smiling countenance to me; but now his smiles were turned into frowns, and his pleasing looks into bended brows: and in rough language, he bade me begone, and tell my tale to the Adigar. Which immediately I did; but he being busy, did not much regard me: and I was glad of it, that I might absent myself from the Court; but I durst not go out of the city [of Digligy]. Sore afraid I was, that evil would befall me; and the best I could expect, was to be put in chains. All my refuge was in prayer to GOD, "whose hand was not shortened that it could not save:" and "would make all things work together for good to them that trust in Him." From Him only did I expect help and deliverance in that time of need.

In this manner, I lodged in an Englishman's house that dwelt in the city, ten days: maintaining myself at my own charge, waiting with a sorrowful heart and daily expecting to hear my doom. In the meantime my countrymen and acquaintance: some of them blamed me for refusing so fair a proffer, whereby I might not only have lived well myself, but also have been helpful unto my poor countrymen and friends; others of them pitying me, suspecting, as I did, nothing but a wrathful sentence from so cruel a tyrant, if GOD did not prevent it. And RICHARD VARNHAM—who was, at this time, a great man about the King—was not a little scared to see me run the hazard of what might ensue; rather than be partaker with him in the felicities of the Court.

It being chargeable thus to lie at the city, and hearing nothing more of my business; I took leave without asking, and went home to my house, which was but a day's distance to get some victuals to carry with me, and to return again. But soon after I came home, I was sent for again; so I took my load of victuals with me, and arrived at the city: but went not to the Court but to my former lodging; where I stayed as formerly, until I had spent all my provisions. And by the good hand of my GOD upon me; I never heard any more of that matter. Neither came I any more into the presence of the great men at Court; but dwelt in my own plantation, upon what GOD provided for me by my labour and industry.

For now I returned to my former course of life: dressing my victuals daily with my own hands, and fetching both wood and water upon mine own back. And this, for ought I could see to the contrary, I was likely to continue for my lifetime. This I could do for the present; but I began to consider how helpless I should be, if it should please GOD that I should live till I grew old and feeble. So I entered upon a consultation with myself for the providing against this. One way was, the getting of me a wife; but that I was resolved never to do. Then I began to inquire for some poor body to live with me; to dress my victuals for me, that

I might live at a little more ease: but could not find any to my mind. Whereupon I considered that there was no better way, than to take one of my poor countrymen's children, whom I might bring up to learn both my own language and religion: and this might be not only charity to the child; but a kindness to myself also afterwards. And several there were that would be glad so to be eased of their charge, having more than they could well maintain. A child therefore I took, by whose aptness, ingenuity and company, as I was much delighted at present; so afterwards I hoped to be served.

It was now about the year 1673. Although I had now lived many years in this land, and, GOD be praised! I wanted for nothing the land afforded; yet I could not forget my native country, England, and lamented under the famine of GOD's Word and Sacraments: the want whereof I found greater than all earthly wants, and my daily and fervent prayers to GOD were, in His good time, to restore me to the enjoyment of them.

I and my companion [STEPHEN RUTLAND] were still meditating upon our escape, and the means to compass it: which our pedling about the country did greatly promote. For speaking well the language, and going with our commodities from place to place; we used often to entertain discourse with the country people, namely, concerning the ways and the countries; and where there were most and fewest inhabitants; and where and how the Watches laid from one country [*district*] to another; and what commodities were proper to carry from one part to the other: pretending we would, from time to time, go from one place to another to furnish ourselves with the wares that the respective places afforded. None doubted but that we had made these inquiries for the sake of our trade; but ourselves had other designs in them: neither was there the least suspicion of us, for these our questions; all supposing I would never run away and leave such an estate as in their accounts and esteem I had.

By diligent inquiry, I had come to understand that the easiest and most probable way to make an escape, was by travelling to the northward: that part of the land being least inhabited. Therefore we furnished ourselves with such wares as were vendible in those parts, as tobacco, pepper, garlic, combs, all sorts of iron ware, &c: and being laden with these things; we two set forth, bending our course towards the northern parts of the island, knowing very little of the way. And the ways of this country generally are intricate and difficult, there being no great highways that run through the land; but a multitude of little paths, some from one town to another, some into the fields, and some into the woods where they sow their corn: and the whole country is covered with woods, so that a man cannot see anything but just before him. And that which makes them most difficult of all is, that the ways shift and alter: new ways being often made and old ways stopped up. For they cut down woods, and sow the ground: and having got one crop off from it, they leave it; and the wood soon grows over it again. And in case a road went through those woods, they stop it, and contrive another way; neither do they regard though it goes two or three miles about. And to ask and inquire the way, was very dangerous for us white men: it occasioning the people to suspect us. And the Cingalese themselves never travel in countries [*districts*] where they are not experienced, without a guide, it being so difficult: and there was no getting a guide to conduct us down to the sea.

But we made a shift to travel from Conde Uda downwards towards the north, from town to town; happening at a place, at last, which I knew before: having been brought up formerly from Coswat that way, to descend the hill called Bocaul; where there is no Watch but in time of great disturbance. Thus, by the providence of God, we passed all difficulties until we came into the country of Nuweeracalava; which are the lowest parts that belong to the King; and some three days' journey from the place whence we came [viz. *Elledat.*]

We were not a little glad that we were gotten so far onwards in our way, but yet at this time we could go no further; for our wares were all sold, and we could pretend no more excuses: and also we had been out so long that it might cause our townsmen to come and look after us; it being the first time that we had been so long absent from home.

In this manner, we went into these northern parts, eight or ten times; and once got as far as Hourly, a town in the extremities of the King's dominions: but yet we could not attain our purpose. For this northern country being much subject to dry weather, and having no springs; we were fain to drink of the ponds of rain water, wherein the cattle lie and tumble: which would be so thick and muddy that the very filth of it would hang in our beards when we drank. This did not agree with our bodies, we being used to drink pure spring water only: by which means, when we first used to visit those parts, we used often to be sick of violent fevers and agues when we came home. Which diseases happened not only to us, but to all other people that dwelt upon the mountains, as we did, whensoever they went down into those places; and commonly the major part of those that fell sick, died. At which the Cingalese were so scared, that it was very seldom that they did adventure their bodies down thither. Neither, truly, would I have done it, were it not for those future hopes; which GOD of His mercy, did at length accomplish. For both of us smarted sufficiently by those severe fevers we got, so that we should both lay sick together, and one not able to help the other: insomuch that our countrymen and neighbours used to ask us, if we went thither purposing to destroy ourselves; they little thinking, and we not daring to tell them of our intent and design.

At length we learned an antidote and counterpoison against the filthy venomous water; which so operated, by the blessing of GOD, that after use thereof, we had no more sickness. It is only a dry leaf—they call it in Portuguese *Banga*—beaten to powder with some of the country's *Jaggery*. And this we ate morning and evening, upon an empty stomach. It intoxicates the brain, and makes one giddy; without any other operation, either by stool or vomit.

Thus every voyage [*journey*] we gathered more experience and got lower down; for this is a large and spacious country. We travelled to and fro where the ways led us; according to their own proverb, *The beggar and the merchant are never out of the way;* because the one begs and the other trades wherever they go. Thus we used to ramble until we had sold all our wares; and then went home for more: and by these means, we grew acquainted both with the people and the paths.

In these parts, I met with my black boy, whom I had divers years before turned away; who had now a wife and children. He proved a great help to me in directing me in the ways; for he had lived many years in these parts. Perceiving him to be able, and also in a very poor and sad condition, not able to maintain his family; I adventured once to ask him if a good reward would not be welcome to him, for guiding us two down to the Dutch; which having done, he might return, and nobody be the wiser. At which proposition he seemed to be very joyful, and promised to undertake the same: only at this time, for reasons he alleged, which to me seemed probable, as that it was harvest time and many people about; it could not so safely and conveniently be done now, as it might be, some two months after.

The business was concluded upon, and the time appointed between us: but it so fell out, that at the very precise time, all things being ready to depart on the morrow; it pleased GOD—whose time was not yet come—to strike me with a most grievous pain in the hollow on my right side, that for five days together I was not able to stir from the fireside; but by warming it and fomenting and chafing it, I got a little ease.

Afterward, as soon as I was recovered and had got strength, we went down, and carried one Englishman more with us for company, for our better security; seeing that we must travel by night upon our flight: but though we took him with us, we dared not to tell him of our design, because he had a wife; intending not to acquaint him with it, till the business was just ready to be put into action. But when we came, expecting to meet with our guide; he was gone into another country: and we knew not where to find him or how to run away without him. Thus we were disappointed that time.

But, as formerly, we went to and fro, until we had sold our ware; and so returned home again, and delivered the man to his wife: but never told him anything of our intended design, fearing lest if he knew it he might acquaint her with it; and so all our purposes coming to be revealed, might be overthrown for ever afterwards. For we were resolved, by GOD's help still to persevere in our design.

Some eight or nine years, one after another, we followed this trade, going into this country on purpose to seek to get beyond the inhabitants; and so to run away through the woods to the Hollanders. Three or four years together, the weather prevented us, when the country was almost starved [*parched*] for want of rain; all which time they never tilled the ground. The wells also were almost all dry, so that in the towns we could scarcely get water to drink or victuals to eat; which affrighted us, at those times, from running into the woods, lest we might perish for thirst. All this while upon the mountains, where our dwelling was, there was no want of rain.

We found it an inconvenience when we came three of us down together; reckoning it might give occasion to the people to suspect our design, and so to prevent us from going thither again. Some of the English as followed such a trade as we did, had been down that way with their commodities: but having felt the smart of that country's sickness, would go there no more; finding as much profit in nearer and easier journeys. But we still persisted in our courses this way, having some greater matter to do here than to sell wares, viz. to find out this Northern Discovery: which, in GOD'S good time, we did effect.

CHAPTER IX.

How the Author began his escape, and got onward of his way, about an hundred miles.

HAving often gone this way to seek for liberty, but could not yet find it; we again set forth, to try what success GOD Almighty would now give us, in the year 1679, on the 22nd of September; furnished with such arms as we could well carry with safety and secrecy, which were knives and small axes: we carried also several sorts of ware to sell as formerly. The moon being seven and twenty days old; which we had so contrived, that we might have a light moon, to see the better to run away by: having left an old man at home, whom I had hired to live with me, to look after my house and goats.

We went down at the hill Bocaul, where there was now no Watch; and but seldom any. From thence, down to the town of Bonder Coswat, where my father died. And by the town of Nicavar, which is the last town belonging to Hotkorle in that road. From thenceforward, the towns stand thin: for it was sixteen miles to the next town, called Parroah, which lay in the country of Nuwerakalawe; and all the way through a wilderness called Parroah Mocolane, full of wild elephants tigers and bears.

Now we set our design for Anuradhapoora, which is the lowest place inhabited belonging to the kingdom of Kandy; where there is a Watch always kept: and nearer than twelve or fourteen miles of this town, as yet, we had never been.

When we came into the midst of this country, we heard that the Governor thereof had sent officers from the Court to dispatch away the King's revenues and duties to the city [of Digligy], and that they were now come into the country: which put us into no small fear, lest if they saw us, they should send us back again. Wherefore we edged away into the westernmost parts of Ecpoulpot, being a remote part of that country, wherein we now were: and there we sat knitting, until we heard they were gone. But this caused us to overshoot our time, the moon spending so fast. As soon as we heard that they were departed out of the country, we went onwards of our journey, having kept most of our wares for a pretence to have an occasion to go further; and having bought a good parcel of cotton yarn to knit caps withal: the rest of our wares, we gave out, was to buy dried flesh with, which only in those lower parts is to be sold.

Our way now lay, necessarily, through the chief Governor's yard at Colliwilla [? *Kalluvilla*]; who dwells there purposely to see and examine all that go and come. This greatly distressed us. First, because he was a stranger to us and one whom we had never seen: and secondly, because there was no other way to escape him; and plain reason would tell him that we, being prisoners, were without our bounds. Whereupon we concluded that our best way would be, to go boldly and resolutely to his house; and not to seem daunted in the least or to look as if we did distrust him to disallow our journey: but to show such a behaviour, as if we had authority to travel where we would.

So we went forward, and were forced to inquire and ask the way to his house, having never been so far this way before. I brought from home with me, knives with fine carved handles and a red Tunis cap, purposely to sell or give to him if occasion required: knowing before, that we must pass by him. And all along as we went, that we might be the less suspected, we sold caps and other wares; to be paid for at our return homewards.

There were many cross paths to and fro, to his house; yet by GOD's providence, we happened in the right road. And having reached his house, according to the country's manner, we went and sat down in the open house; which kind of houses are built on purpose for the reception of strangers. Whither, not long after, the great man himself came and sat down by us; to whom we presented a small parcel of tobacco, and some betel. And before he asked us the cause of our coming; we showed him the wares we brought for him, and the cotton yarn we had trucked about the country, telling him withal, how the case stood with us, viz: "That we had a charge greater than the King's allowance would maintain, and that because dried flesh was the chief commodity of that part;" we told him "that missing of the lading which we used to carry back, we were glad to come thither to see if we could make it up with dried flesh: and therefore if he would please to supply us—either for such wares as we had brought or else for our money—it would be a great favour; the which would oblige us for the future to bring him any necessaries that he should name unto us, when we should come again into those parts, as we used to do very often; and that we could furnish him, having dealings and being acquainted with the best artificers in Kandy."

At which he replied, "That he was sorry we were come at such a dry time, when they could not catch deer; but if some rain fell, he would soon dispatch us with some ladings of flesh: but however he bade us go about the towns and see whether there might be any or not, though he thought there was none." This answer of his pleased us wondrously well; both because by this we saw he suspected us not, and because he told us there was no dried flesh to be got. For it was one of our greatest fears that we should get our lading too soon; for then we could not have had an excuse to go further: and as yet we could not possibly fly; having still six miles further to the northward to go, before we could attempt it, that is, to Anuradhapoora.

From Anuradhapoora, it is two days' journey further through a desolate wilderness, before there are any more inhabitants: and these inhabitants are neither under this King nor the Dutch; but are Malabars, and are under a Prince of their own. This people we were sorely afraid of, lest they might seize us and send us back: there being a correspondence between this Prince and the King of Kandy: wherefore it was our endeavour by all means to shun them, lest, according to the old proverb, we might leap out of the fryingpan into the fire.

But we must take care of that as well as we could, when we came among them; for as yet our care was to get to Anuradhapoora, where although it was our desire to get, yet we would not seem to be too hasty, lest it might occasion suspicion, but lay where we were two or three days: and one stayed at the Governor's house a knitting; whilst the other went about among the towns to see for flesh. The ponds in the country being now dry, there was fish everywhere in abundance; which they dry like red herrings over a fire. They offered to sell us a store of them; "but they," we told them, "would not turn to so good profit as flesh." "The which," we said, "we would have, though we stayed ten days longer for it. For here we could live as cheap, and earn as much as if we were at home, by our knitting." So we seemed to them as if we were not in any haste.

In the meantime happened an accident which put us to a great fright. For the King, having newly clapped up several persons of quality (whereof my old neighbour OWA MOTTERAL that sent for me to Court, was one) sent down soldiers to this High Sheriff or Governor at whose house we now were, to give him order to set a secure guard at the Watches that no suspicious persons might pass. This he did to prevent the relations of these imprisoned persons from making an escape; who—through fear of the King—might attempt it. This always is the King's custom to do. But it put us into an exceeding fear lest it might beget an admiration [*wonderment*] in these soldiers to see white men so low down the country; which indeed is not customary nor allowed of; and so they might send us up again. Which doubtless they would have done; had it not been of GOD by this means and after this manner to deliver us. Especially considering that the King's command came just at that time, and so expressly to keep a secure guard at the Watches, and that in that very way that always we purposed to go in; so that it seemed scarcely possible for us to pass afterwards: though we should get off fairly at present with the soldiers. Which we did. For they having delivered their message, departed; showing themselves very kind and civil unto us: and we seemed to lament for our hard fortune, that we were not ready to go upwards with them, in their good company: for we were neighbours dwelling in one and the same country. However we bade them carry our commendations to our countrymen the English—with whom they were acquainted at the city—and so bade them farewell. And glad we were when they were gone from us: and we resolved, GOD willing, to set forward the next day in the morning.

But we thought not fit to tell our host, the Governor, of it, till the very instant of our departure; that he might not have any time to deliberate concerning us. That night, he, being disposed to be merry, sent for people whose trade it is to dance and show tricks, to come to his house, to entertain him with their sports. The beholding of them spent most part of the night: which we merely called our old host's civility to us at our last parting; as it proved indeed, though he, honest man, then little dreamed of any such thing.

The morning being come, we first took care to fill our bellies; then we packed up those things which were necessary for our journey to carry with us; and the rest of our goods—cotton yarn, cloth, and other things—that we would not incumber ourselves withal, we bound up in a bundle, intending to leave them behind us. This being done, I went to the Governor, and carried to him four or five charges of gunpowder, a thing somewhat scarce with them; intreating him rather than that we should be disappointed of flesh; to make use of that and shoot some deer—which he was very willing to accept of; and to us it could be no ways profitable, not having a gun—while we, we told him, "would make a step to Anuradhapoora to see what flesh we could procure there." In the meantime, according as we had before laid the business, came STEPHEN RUTLAND with the bundle of goods, desiring to leave them in his house, till we came back: which he was very ready to grant us leave to do. And seeing us leave such a parcel of goods—though, GOD knows, but of little account in themselves, yet of considerable value in that land—he could not suppose otherwise but that we were intending to return again. Thus we took our leave and immediately departed, not giving him time again to consider with himself, or to consult with others about us: and he, like a good-natured man, bade us heartily farewell.

Although we knew not the way to this town—having never been there in all our lives; and durst not ask, lest it might breed suspicion—yet we went on confidently through a desolate wood; and happened to go very right, and came out directly at the place.

But in our way, before we arrived thither, we came up with a small river, which ran through the woods, called by the Cingalese, Malwatta Oya: the which we viewed well and judged it might be a probable guide to carry us down to the sea; if a better did not present itself. However we thought good to try first the way we were taking, and to go onwards towards Anuradhapoora, that being the shortest and easiest way to get to the coast, and this river, being as under our lee, ready to serve and assist us, if other means failed.

To Anuradhapoora, called also Neur Wang, therefore we came; which is not so much a particular single town, as a territory. It is a vast great plain—the like of which I never saw in all that island—in the midst whereof is a lake, which may be a mile over; not natural, but made by art as are the other ponds in the country, to serve them to water their corn grounds. This plain is encompassed round with woods, and small towns among them on every side inhabited by Malabars, a distinct race from the Cingalese: but these towns we could not see, till we came in among them.

Being come through the woods into this plain, we stood looking and staring round about us: but knew not where nor which way to go. At length, we heard a cock crow, which was a sure sign to us that there was a town hard by; into which we were resolved to enter. For standing thus amazed was the ready way to be taken up for suspicious persons; especially because white men never came down so low.

Being entered into the town, we sat ourselves under a tree, and proclaimed our wares: for we feared to rush into their yards as we used to do in other places, lest we should scare them. The people stood amazed, as soon as they saw us; being originally Malabars, though subjects of Kandy: nor could they understand the Cingalese language in which we spake to them. And we stood looking one upon another, until there came one that could speak the Cingalese tongue, who asked us, "From whence we came?" We told him from Conde Uda: but they believed us not, supposing that we came up from the Dutch, from Manaar. So they brought us before their Governor. He not speaking Cingalese, spake to us by an interpreter; and to know the truth whether we came from the place we pretended, he inquired about the news at Court: and demanded "who were Governors of such and such countries?" and "What was become of some certain noblemen?" (whom the King had lately cut off) and also "What the common people were employed about at Court?" for it is seldom that they are idle. To all which, we gave satisfactory answers. Then he inquired of us "Who gave us leave to come down so low?" We told him, "That privilege was given to us by the King himself full fifteen years since at his palace at Nellembe; when he caused it to be declared unto us that we were no longer prisoners, and," which indeed was our own addition, "that we were free to enjoy the benefit of trade in all his dominions."

To prove and confirm the truth of which, we alleged the distance of the way that we were now come from home, being nearly an hundred miles, passing through several counties, where we met with several Governors and Officers in their respective jurisdictions; who, had they not been well sensible of these privileges granted to us, would not have allowed us to pass through their countries [*districts*]. All which Officers we described to them by name. And also that now we came from the High Sheriff's house at Colliwilla, where we had been these three days, and there heard of the order that was come to secure the Watches; which was not for fear of the running away of white men, but of the Cingalese. These reasons gave him full satisfaction, that we were innocent traders: seeing also the commodities that we had brought with us; this further confirmed his opinion concerning us.

The people were very glad of our coming, and gave us an end of an open house to lie in: but at present they had no dried flesh, but desired us to stay two or three days, and we should not fail: which we were very ready to consent to, hoping by that time to come to the knowledge of the way, and to learn where about the Watch was placed. To prevent the least surmise that we were plotting to run away; we agreed that STEPHEN RUTLAND should stay in the house by the things; while I, with some few of them, went abroad, pretending to inquire for dried flesh to carry back with us to Kandy, but intending to make discoveries of the way, and to provide necessaries for our flight, as rice, a brass pot to boil our rice in, a little dried flesh to eat, and a deerskin to make us shoes of. And by the providence of my gracious GOD, all these things I happened upon, and bought: but, as our good hap was, of deer's flesh we could meet with none. So that we had time enough to fit ourselves; all people thinking that we stayed only to buy flesh.

Here we stayed three days. During which, we had found the great road that runs down towards Jaffnapatam, one of the northern ports belonging to the Dutch: which road, we judged led also towards Manaar, a Dutch northern port also, which was the place that we endeavoured to get to; it lying about two or three days' journey distant from us. But in this road there was a Watch laid which must be passed. Where this Watch was placed, it was necessary for us punctually [*precisely*] to know, and to endeavour to get a sight of it: and if we could do this, our intent was to go unseen by night —the people being then afraid to travel—and being come up to the Watch, to slip aside into the woods, and so go on until we were passed it; and then to strike into the road again. But this project came to nothing, because I could not without suspicion and danger, go and view this Watch; which lay some four or five miles below this plain: and so far I could not frame any business to go.

But several inconveniences we saw here. insomuch that we found it would not be safe for us to go down in this road. For if we should have slipped away from them by night; in the morning, we should be missed: and then most surely, they would go that way to chase us; and, ten to one, overtake us, being but one night before them. Also we knew not whether or not, it might lead us into the country of the Malabar Prince; of whom we were much afraid.

Then resolving to let the great road alone, we thought of going right down through the woods, and steer our course by the sun and moon; but the ground being so dry, we feared we should not meet with water. So we declined that counsel also.

Thus being in doubt, we prayed to GOD to direct us, and to put it into our heads which way to take. Then, after a consultation between ourselves, all things considered, we concluded it to be the best course to go back to Malwatta Oya; the river that we had well viewed, and that lay in our way as we came hither.

CHAPTER X.

The Author's progress in his flight from Anuradhapoora into the woods; until their arrival in the Malabars' country.

NOW GOD, of His mercy, having prospered our design hitherto, for which we blessed His holy name; our next care was how to come off clear from the people of Anuradhapoora, that they might not presently miss us, and so pursue after us: which if they should do, there would have been no escaping them. For from this town to Colliwilla—where the Sheriff lived, with whom we left our goods—they were as well acquainted in the woods as in the paths: and when we came away, we must tell the people that we were going thither; because there was no other way but that. Now our fear was lest upon some occasion or other, any men might chance to travel that way soon after we were gone; and not finding us at Colliwilla might conclude, as they could do no otherwise, that we were run into the woods. Therefore to avoid this danger, we stayed in the town till it was so late that we knew that none durst venture to travel afterwards, for fear of wild beasts. By which means we were sure to gain a night's travel, at least: if they should chance to pursue us.

So we took our leaves of the Governor, who kindly gave us a pot of milk to drink, for a farewell: we telling him, "We were returning back to the Sheriff at Colliwilla, to whom we had given some gunpowder when we came from him, to shoot us some deer: and we doubted not but by that time we should get to him, he would have provided flesh enough for our lading home." Thus bidding him and the rest of the neighbours farewell, we departed: they giving us the civility of their accustomed prayers; *Diabac*, that is, "God bless or keep you."

It was now the 12th day of October on a Sunday, the moon eighteen days old. We were well furnished with all things needful, which we could get, viz.—ten days' provisions, rice, flesh, fish, pepper, salt; a basin to boil our victuals in; two calabashes to fetch water; two great Tallipat [leaves] for tents, big enough to sleep under, if it should rain; *Jaggery* and sweetmeats, which we brought from home with us; tobacco also and betel; tinder boxes, two or three for fear of failing; and a deer's skin to make us shoes, to prevent any thorns running into our feet as we travelled through the woods, for our greatest trust, under GOD, was to our feet. Our weapons were, to each man a small axe fastened to a long staff in our hands, and a good knife by our sides: which were sufficient, with GOD's help, to defend us from the assaults of either tiger or bear; and as for elephants, there is no standing against them, but the best defence is to fly from them.

In this posture and equipage we marched forward. When we were come within a mile of this river, it being about four in the evening, we began to fear lest any of the people of Anuradhapoora from whence we came, should follow us to Colliwilla; which place we never intended to come at more: the river along which we intended to go, laying on this side of it. That we might be secure therefore, that no people came after us; we sat down upon a rock by a hole that was full of water in the highway, until it was so late that we were sure no people durst travel. In case any had come after us, and seen us sitting there, and gotten no further; we intended to tell them that one of us was taken sick by the way, and therefore was not able to go on. But it was our happy chance, that there came none.

So about sundown, we took up our sacks of provisions, and marched forward for the river; which, under GOD, we had pitched upon to be our guide down to the sea.

Being come at the river; we left the road, and struck into the woods by the river side. We were exceedingly careful not to tread on the sand or soft ground, lest our footsteps should be seen: and where it could not be avoided, we went backwards; so that by the print of our feet it seemed as if we had gone the contrary way. We had now got a good way into the wood, when it grew dark and began to rain; so that we thought it best to pitch our tents, and get wood for firing before it was all wet, and too dark to find it: which we did, and kindled a fire.

Then we began to fit ourselves for our journey, against the moon rose. All our sale-wares which we had left, we cast away, for we had taken care not to sell too much; keeping only provisions, and what was very necessary for our journey. About our feet we tied pieces of deer's-hide, to prevent thorns and stumps annoying our feet. We always used to travel barefoot, but now being to travel by night and in the woods, we feared to do so: for if our feet should fail us now, we were quite undone.

And by the time we had well fitted ourselves, and were refreshed with a morsel of Portuguese sweetmeats; the moon began to shine. So having commended ourselves into the hands of the Almighty, we took up our provisions upon our shoulders and set forward, and travelled some three or four hours, but with a great deal of difficulty. For the trees being thick, the moon gave us but little light through: but our resolution was, to keep going.

Now it was our chance to meet with an elephant in our way, just before us; which we tried to, but could not scare away: so he forced us to stay. We kindled a fire and sat down; and took a pipe of tobacco, waiting till morning. Then we looked round about us, and it appeared all like a wilderness, and no signs that people ever had been there; which put us in great hopes that we had gained our passage, and were past all the inhabitants. Whereupon we concluded that we were now in no danger of being seen, and might travel in the day securely.

There was only one great road in our way, which led to Portaloon from the towns which by and by we fell into. This road therefore we were shy of; lest when we passed it over, some passengers travelling on it, might see us. And this road we were in expectance about this time, to meet withal, feeling secure, as I said before, of all other danger of people: but the river winding about to the northward, brought us into the midst of a parcel of towns, called Tissea Wava, before we were aware of it. For the country being all woods, we could not discern where there were towns until we came within the hearing of them. That which betrayed us into this danger was, that meeting with a path which only led from one town to another, we concluded it to be that great road above mentioned, and so having passed it over;

we supposed the danger we might encounter in being seen was also passed over with it: but we were mistaken, for going further we still met with other paths, which we crossed over, still hoping one or other of them was that great road; but at last we perceived our error, namely, that they were only paths that went from one town to another.

And so while we were avoiding men and towns, we ran into the midst of them. This was a great trouble to us; hearing the noise of people round about us, and not knowing how to avoid them: into whose hands we knew if we should have fallen; they would have carried us up to the King, besides beating and plundering us to boot.

We knew before, that these towns were here away: but had we known that this river turned and ran in among them; we should never have undertaken the enterprise. But now to go back, after we had newly passed so many paths, and fields, and places, where people did resort: we thought it not advisable, and that the danger in so doing might be greater than in going forward. And had we known so much then as afterwards did appear to us; it had been safer for us to have gone on, than to have hid as we did: which we then thought the best course we could take for the present extremity, viz.—to secure ourselves in secret until night, and then to run through, in the dark. All that we wanted was a hole to creep in, to lie close: for the woods thereabouts were thin, and there were no shrubs or bushes, under which we might be concealed.

We heard the noise of people on every side, and expected every moment to see some of them: to our great terror. And it is not easy to say, in what danger; and in what apprehension of it we were. It was not safe for us to stir backwards or forwards, for fearing of running among the people; and it was as unsafe to stand still, where we were, lest somebody might spy us: and where to find covert, we could not tell.

Looking about us, in these straits, we spied a great tree by us, which for the bigness thereof 'twas probable might be hollow. To which we went, and found it so. It was like a tub, some three feet high. Into it, immediately we both crept, and made a shift to sit there for several hours, though very uneasily, and all in mud and wet. But however it did great comfort us, in the fright and amazement we were in.

So soon as it began to grow dark, we came creeping out of our hollow tree; and put for it, as fast as our legs could carry us. And then we crossed that great road, which all the day before we did expect to come up with; keeping close by the river side; and going so long, till dark night stopped us.

We kept going the longer, because we heard the voice of men holloaing towards evening; which created in us a fresh disturbance: thinking them to be people that were coming to chase us. But at length; we heard elephants behind us, between us and the voice, which we knew by the noise of the cracking of the boughs and small trees which they brake down and ate. These elephants were a very good guard behind us; and were, methought, like the darkness that came between Israel and the Egyptians. For the people, we knew, would not dare to go forwards; hearing elephants before them.

In this security, we pitched our tents by the river side, and boiled rice and roasted flesh for our supper: for we were very hungry; and so, commending ourselves to GOD's keeping, we lay down to sleep. The voice which we heard still continued; which lasting so long, we knew what it meant. It was nothing but the holloaing of people that lay to watch the cornfields; to scare away the wild beasts out of their corn.

Thus we passed Monday.

But nevertheless the next morning, so soon as the moon shone out bright; to prevent the worst, we took up our packs, and were gone: being past all the tame inhabitants, with whom we had no more trouble.

But the next day, we feared we should come among the wild ones: for these woods are full of them. Of these, we were as much afraid as of the other: for they [*the tame inhabitants*] would have carried us back to the King, where we should have been kept prisoners; but these, we feared, would have shot us, not standing to hear us plead for ourselves.

And indeed all along as we went, by the sides of the river, till we came to the Malabar inhabitants; there had been the tents of wild men, made only of boughs of trees. But GOD be praised, they were all gone: though but very lately before we came; as we perceived by the bones of cattle and shells of fruit, which lay scattered about. We supposed that want of water had driven them out of the country down to the river side; but that since it had rained a shower or two, they were gone again.

Once, about noon, sitting down upon a rock by the river side to take a pipe of tobacco and rest ourselves; we had almost been discovered by the women of these wild people: coming down, as I suppose, to wash themselves in the river; who, being many of them, came talking and laughing together. At the first hearing of the noise, being at a good distance, we marvelled what it was. Sitting still and listening; it came a little above where we sat: and at last, we could plainly distinguish it to be the voices of women and children. Whereupon we thought it no boot to sit longer, since we could escape unobserved; and so took up our bags, and fled as fast as we could.

Thus we kept travelling every day, from morning till night, still along by the river side, which turned and wound very crookedly. In some places, it would be pretty good travelling and but few bushes and thorns; in others, a great many: so that our shoulders and arms were all of a gore, being grievously torn and scratched. For we had nothing on us, but a clout round about our middles, and our victuals on our shoulders; and in our hands, a tallipat [palm leaf] and an axe.

The lower we came down this river, the less water; so that sometimes we could go a mile or two upon the sand. And in some places, three or four rivers would all meet together. When this happened so, and was noon—the sun over our head, and the water not running—we could not tell which to follow; but were forced to stay till the sun was fallen, thereby to judge our course.

We often met with bears, hogs, deer and wild buffaloes; but they all ran, so soon as they saw us: but elephants we met with no more than that I have mentioned before. The river is exceeding full of alligators all along as we went: and the upper part of it is nothing but rocks.

Here and there, by the side of this river, there is a world of hewn stone pillars, standing upright; and other heaps of hewn stones, which I suppose formerly were buildings. And in three or four places, are the ruins of bridges, built of stone; some remains of them yet standing upon stone pillars. In many places are points built out into the river, like wharves; all of hewn stone: which I suppose have been built for kings to sit upon for pleasure; for I cannot think they ever were employed for traffic by water, the river being so full of rocks that boats could never come up into it.

The woods in all these northern parts are short and shrubbed; and so they are here by the river's side: and the lower down the river, the worse; and the grounds so also.

In the evenings we used to pitch our tent, and make a great fire, both before and behind us; that the wild beasts might have notice where we lay: and we used to hear the voices of all sorts of them; but, thanks be to GOD! none ever came near to hurt us.

Yet we were the more wary of them; because once a tiger showed us a cheat. For having bought a deer (and having nothing to salt it up in) we packed it up in the hide thereof salted, and laid it under a bench in an open house, on which bench I lay that night; and STEPHEN lay just by it on the ground; and some three people more lay then in the same house; and in the said house there was a great fire; and another in the yard: yet a tiger came in the night, and carried deer and hide and all away. But we missing it; concluded that it was a thief that had done it. We called up the people that lay by us; and told them what had happened; who informed us that it was a tiger; and with a torch, they went to see which way he had gone, and presently found some of it, which he had let drop by the way. When it was day, we went further; and picked up more, which was scattered; till we came to the hide itself, which remained uneaten.

We had now travelled till Thursday afternoon, when we crossed the river called Coronda Oya [? *Kannadera Oya*], which was then quite dry. This parts the King's country from that of the Malabars. We saw no sign of inhabitants here. The woods began to be very full of thorns and shrubby bushes, with cliffs and broken land; so that we could not possibly go in the woods. But now the river grew better, being clear of rocks; and dry, water only standing in holes. So we marched along in the river bed upon the sand. Hereabouts are far more elephants than higher up. By day, we saw none; but by night, the river was full of them.

On Friday, about nine or ten in the morning, we came among the inhabitants: for then we saw the footing [*footprints*] of people on the sand; and tame cattle with bells about their necks. Yet we kept on our way right down the river; knowing no other course to take, to shun the people. And as we went still forwards, we saw coracan corn sown in the woods; but neither town, nor people, nor so much as the voice of man: yet we were somewhat dismayed; knowing that we were now in a country inhabited by Malabars.

The *Wanniounay* or Prince of this people for fear, pays tribute to the Dutch ; but stands far more affected towards the King of Kandy: which made our care the greater to keep ourselves out of his hands; fearing lest if he did not keep us himself, he might send us up to our old master. So that great was our terror again, lest meeting with people we might be discovered.

Yet there was no means now left us how to avoid the danger of being seen. The woods were so bad that we could not possibly travel in them for thorns; and to travel by night was impossible, it being a dark moon; and the river at night so full of elephants and other wild beasts coming to drink, as we did both hear and see, lying upon the banks with a fire by us. They came in such numbers, because there was water for them nowhere else to be had: the ponds and holes of water; nay the river itself, in many places being dry. There was therefore no other way to be taken, but to travel on in the river.

So down we went into the sand and put on as fast as we could set our legs to the ground: seeing no people, nor, I think, nobody us; but only buffaloes in abundançe in the water.

CHAPTER XI.

Being in the Malabar territories; how they encountered two men, and what passed between them. And of their getting safe unto the Dutch fort; and their reception there, and at the Island of Manaar; until their embarking for Colombo.

THUS we went on till about three o'clock in the afternoon. At which time, coming about a point, we came up with two Brahmins on a sudden; who were sitting under a tree, boiling rice. We were within forty paces of them. When they saw us they were amazed at us; and as much afraid of us, as we were of them. Now we thought it better policy to treat with them, than to fly from them: fearing they might have bows and arrows, whereas we were armed only with axes in our hands, and knives by our sides; or else that they might raise the country and pursue us. So we made a stand, and in the Cingalese language, asked their leave to come near and treat with them, but they did not understand it: but being risen up, spake to us in the Malabar tongue, which we could not understand. Then, still standing at a distance, we intimated our minds to them by signs, beckoning with our hand: which they answered in the same language.

Then offering to go towards them, and seeing them to be naked men, and no arms near them; we laid our axes upon the ground with our bags: lest we might scare them, if we had come up to them with those weapons in our hands; and so went towards them with only our knives by our sides.

By signs with our hands, showing them our bloody backs; we made understand whence we came, and whither we were going: which when they perceived, they seemed to commiserate our condition, and greatly to admire at such a miracle which GOD had brought to pass; and as they talked one to another, they lifted up their hands and faces towards heaven, after repeating *Tombrane*, which is *God* in the Malabar tongue.

And by their signs, we understood they would have us bring our bags and axes nearer: which we had no sooner done; but they brought the rice and herbs which they had boiled for themselves to us, and bade us eat; which we were not fitted to do, having not long before eaten a hearty dinner of better fare. Yet we could not but thankfully accept of their compassion and kindness, and eat as much as we could; and in requital of their courtesy, we gave them some of our tobacco: which, after much entreating, they did receive, and it pleased them exceedingly.

After these civilities passed on either side; we began by signs to desire them to go with us, and show us the way to the Dutch fort: which they were very unwilling to do, saying—as by signs and some few words which we could understand—that our greatest danger was past; and that by night, we might get into the Hollanders' dominions.

Yet we being weary with our tedious journey, and desirous to have a guide; showed them money to the value of five shillings, being all I had, and offered it to them, to go with us. Which together with our great importunity, so prevailed, that one of them took it; and leaving his fellow to carry their baggage, he went with us about one mile, and then began to take his leave of us and to return: which we supposed was to get more from us. Having therefore no more money, we gave him a red Tunis cap and a knife; for which he went a mile further, and then as before would leave us, signifying to us, "that we were out of danger, and he could go no farther."

Now we had no more left to give him; but began to perceive that what we had parted withal to him was but flung away. And although we might have taken all from him again, being alone in the wood; yet we feared to do it, lest thereby we might exasperate him, and so he might give notice of us to the people: but bade him farewell; after he had conducted us four or five miles.

We kept on our journey down the river as before, until it was night; and lodged upon a bank under a tree: but were in the way of the elephants; for in the night they came and had like to have disturbed us; so that for our preservation we were forced to fling firebrands at them to scare them away.

The next morning, being Saturday, as soon as it was light, having eaten to strengthen us (as horses do oats before they travel), we set forth, going still down. The sand was dry and loose and so very tedious to go upon, by the side of the river we could not go, it being all overgrown with bushes. The land hereabouts was as smooth as a bowling green; but the grass clean burnt up for want of rain.

Having travelled about two hours, we saw a man walking in the river before, whom we would gladly have shunned, but well could not: for he walked down the river as we did: but at a very slow rate, which much hindered us. But considering upon the distance we had come since we left the Brahmin and comparing with what he told us, we concluded we were in the Hollanders' jurisdiction; and so amended our pace to overtake the man before us: whom we perceiving to be free from timorousness at the sight of us, concluded he had been used to see white men.

Whereupon, we asked him, "to whom he belonged?" He, speaking the Cingalese language, answered, "to the Dutch;" and also "that all the country was under their command, and that we were out of danger, and that the fort of Aripo was but some six miles off." Which did not a little rejoice us. We told him, "we were of that nation, and had made our escape from Kandy, where we had been many years kept in captivity:" and—having nothing to give him ourselves—we told him, "that it was not to be doubted, but that the chief Commander at the fort would bountifully reward him if he would go with us, and direct us thither." But whether he doubted of that or not, or whether he expected something in hand; he excused himself, pretending earnest and urgent occasions that he could not defer. But he advised us to leave the river, because it winds so much about, and to turn up without fear to the towns; where the people would direct us the way to the fort.

Upon his advice, we struck up a path that came down to the river, intending to go to a town, but could find none: and there were so many cross paths that we could not tell which way to go; and the land here was so exceedingly low and level, that we could see no other thing but trees. For although I got up a tree to look if I could see the Dutch fort or discern any houses; yet I could not: and the sun being right over our heads, neither could that direct us. Insomuch that we wished ourselves again in our old friend, the river. So after much wandering up and down; we sat down under a tree, waiting until the sun was fallen or some people came by.

Which not long after, three or four Malabars did. We told these men that we were Hollanders: supposing they would be the more willing to go with us; but they proved of the same temper with the rest before mentioned. For until I gave one of them a small knife to cut betel nuts, he would not go with us; but for the lucre of that, he conducted us to a town. From whence, they sent a man with us to the next. And so we were passed from town to town, until we arrived at the fort called Aripo. It being about four o'clock on Saturday afternoon, October the 18th, 1679.

Which day, GOD grant us grace that we may never forget: when He was pleased to give us so great a deliverance from such a long captivity of nineteen years, and six months, and odd days: I being taken prisoner when I was nineteen years old; and continued upon the mountains among the heathen till I attained to eight and thirty.

In this flight through the woods; I cannot but take notice with some wonder and great thankfulness, that this travelling by night in a desolate wilderness was little or nothing dreadful to me; whereas formerly the very thoughts of it would seem to dread me. And in the night, when I lay down to rest, with wild beasts round me; I slept as soundly and securely as ever I did at home in my own house. Which courage and peace, I look upon to be the immediate gift of GOD to me, upon my earnest prayers; which at that time he poured into my heart in great measure and fervency. After which I found myself freed from those frights and fears, which usually possessed my heart at other times.

In short, I look upon the whole business as a miraculous providence; and that the hand of GOD did eminently appear to me as it did of old to his people Israel in the like circumstances; in leading and conducting me through this dreadful wilderness, and not to suffer any evil to approach nigh unto me.

The Hollanders much wondered at our arrival—it being so strange that any should escape from Kandy—and entertained us very kindly that night.

And the next morning, being Sunday; they sent a Corporal with us to Manaar, and a black man to carry our few things.

At Manaar, we were brought before the Captain of the castle, the Chief Governor being absent; who, when we came in, was just risen from dinner. He received us with a great deal of kindness, and bade us sit down to eat.

It seemed not a little strange to us, who had dwelt so long in straw cottages among the black heathen, and used to sit on the ground, and eat our meat on leaves; now to sit on chairs, and eat out of china dishes at a table; where there were great varieties, and a fair and sumptuous house inhabited by white and Christian people: we being then in such habit and guise (our natural colour excepted) that we seemed not fit to eat with his servants, no, nor his slaves.

After dinner, the Captain inquired concerning the affairs of the King and country, and the condition of their Ambassadors and people there. To all which, we gave them true and satisfactory answers. Then he told us "that to-morrow, there was a sloop to sail to Jaffnapatam, in which he would send us to the Commander and Governor; from whence we might have a passage to Fort Saint George [*Madras*] or any other place on that coast, according to our desire." After this, he gave us some money; bidding us go to the Castle to drink, and be merry with our countrymen there. For all which kindness, giving him many thanks in the Portuguese language; we took our leaves of him.

When we came to the court of guard at the Castle; we asked the soldiers if there were no Englishmen among them. Immediately there came forth two men to us, the one a Scotchman named ANDREW BROWN; the other an Irishman, whose name was FRANCIS HODGES: who, after very kind salutes, carried us unto their lodgings in the castle; and entertained us very nobly, according to their ability, with arrack and tobacco.

The news of our arrival being spread in the town, the people came flocking to see us as a strange and wonderful sight: and some to inquire about their husbands, sons and relations which were prisoners at Kandy.

In the evening a gentlemen of the town sent to invite us to his house; where we were gallantly entertained both with victuals and lodging.

The next day, being Monday, while ready to embark for Jaffnapatam; there came an order from the Captain and Council that we must stay until the Commander of Jaffnapatam, who was daily expected, came thither: which we could not deny to do; and order was given to the Victuallers of the soldiers to provide for us. The Scotchman and Irishman were very glad of this order, that they might have our company longer: and would not suffer us to spend the Captain's benevolence in their company, but spent freely upon us at their own charges.

Thanks be to GOD, we both continued in health all the time of our escape; but within three days after we came to Manaar, my companion fell very sick; so that I thought I should have lost him.

Thus we remained some ten days. At which time the expected Commander arrived, and was received with great ceremonies of state. The next day we went before him, to receive his orders concerning us: which were to be ready to go with him on the morrow to Colombo; there being a ship, that had long waited in that road to carry him. In which, we embark with him for Colombo.

At our coming on board to go to sea, we could not expect but to be seasick; being now as fresh men having so long disused the sea: but it proved otherwise, and we were not in the least stirred.

CHAPTER XII.

Their arrival at Colombo and entertainment there. Their departure thence to Batavia; and from thence to Bantam: whence they set sail for England.

BEING safely arrived at Colombo, before the ship came to an anchor; there came a barge on board to carry the Commander ashore. But it being late in the evening, and my consort being sick of an ague and fever; we thought it better for us to stay on board until the morning, so as to have a day before us.

The next morning, we bade the skipper farewell, and went ashore in the first boat: going straight to the Court of Guard; where all the soldiers came staring upon us, wondering to see white men in Cingalese habits. We asked them, if "there were no Englishmen among them." They told us, "there were none, but that in the city there were several." A trumpeter being hard by who had formerly sailed in English ships; hearing of us, came and invited us to his chamber: and entertained my consort being sick of his ague, in his own bed.

The strange news of our arrival from Kandy was presently spread all about the city, and all the Englishmen that were there immediately came to bid us welcome out of our long captivity: with whom we consulted how to come to speech of the Governor. Upon which, one of them went and acquainted the Captain of the Guard of our being on shore; which the Captain understanding, went and informed the Governor thereof. Who sent us answer that to-morrow we should come before him.

After my consort's fit was over; our countrymen and their friends invited us abroad to walk and see the city. We being barefooted and in Cingalese habit with great long beards; the people much wondered at us, and came flocking to see who and what we were; so that we had a great train of people about us, as we walked in the streets. And after we had walked to and fro, and had seen the city; they carried us to their landlady's house, where we were kindly treated both with victuals and drink; and returned to the trumpeter's house as he had desired us when we went out. In the evening, came a boy from the Governor's house to tell us, that the Governor invited us to come to supper at his house: but we—having dined lately with our countrymen and their friends—had no room to receive the Governor's kindness; and so lodged that night, at the trumpeter's.

The next morning, the Governor—whose name was RICKLOF VAN GONS, son of RICKLOF VAN GONS the General of Batavia—sent for us to his house. Whom we found standing in a large and stately room, paved with black and white stones: and only the Commander of Jaffnapatam, who brought us from Manaar, standing by him; who was to succeed him in the government of that place. On the further side of the room, stood three of the chief Captains bareheaded.

First, "he bade us welcome out of our long captivity," and told us "That we were free men: and that he should have been glad if he could have been an instrument to redeem us sooner; having endeavoured as much for us as for his own people." For all which, we thanked him heartily: telling him, "We knew it to be true."

The Governor perceiving I could speak the Portuguese tongue, began to inquire concerning the affairs of the King and country very particularly; and oftentimes asked about such matters as he himself knew better than I. To all his questions, my too much experience enabled me to give a satisfactory reply. Some of the most remarkable matters he demanded of me, were these.

First, they inquired much about the reason and intent of our coming to Kottiaar: to which, I answered them at large.

Then they asked, "If the King of Kandy had any issue?" I told them, "As report went, he had none."

And, "Who were the greatest in the realm, next to him?" I answered, "There were none of renown left, the King had destroyed them all."

"How the hearts of the people stood affected?" I answered, "Much against their King: he being so cruel."

"If we had never been brought into his presence?" I told them, "No, nor never had had a near sight of him."

"What strength he had for war?" I answered, "Not well able to assault them, by reason that the hearts of his people were not true to him: but that the strength of his country consisted in mountains and woods, as much as in the people."

"What army could he raise upon occasion?" I answered, "I knew not well; but, as I thought, about thirty thousand men."

"Why would he not make peace with them: they so much suing for it, and sending presents to please him?" I answered, "I was not one of his Council, and knew not his meaning."

But they demanded of me, "What I thought might be the reason or occasion of it?" I answered, "Living securely in the mountains, he feareth none; and for traffic, he regardeth it not."

"Which way was best and most secure to send spies or intelligence to Kandy?" I told them, "By the way that goeth to Jaffnapatam; and by some of that country's people, who have great correspondence with the people of Nuwerakalawe, one of the King's countries."

"What I thought would become of that land after the King's decease?" I told them, "I thought, he having no issue; it might fall into their hands."

"How many Englishmen had served the King, and what became of them?" Which I gave them an account of.

"Whether I had an acquaintance or discourse with the great men at Court?" I answered, "That I was too small to have any friendship or intimacy or hold discourse with them."

"How the common people used to talk concerning them [*the Dutch*]?" I answered, "They used much to commend their justice and good government in the territories and over the people belonging unto them."

"Whether the King did take counsel of any, or rule and act only by his own will and pleasure?" I answered, "I was a stranger at Court, and how could I know that?"

"But," they asked further, "what was my opinion?" I replied, "He is so great, that there is none great enough to give him counsel."

Concerning the French: "if the King knew not of their coming, before they came?" I answered, "I thought not, because their coming seemed strange and wonderful unto the people."

"How they had proceeded in treating with the King?" I answered as shall be related hereafter, when I come to speak of the French detained in this land.

"If I knew any way or means to be used, whereby the prisoners in Kandy might be set free?" I told them, "Means I knew none, unless they could do it by war."

Also they inquired about the manner of executing those whom the King commands to be put to death. They inquired also very curiously concerning the manner of our surprisal, and entertainment or usage among them; and in what parts of the land, we had our residence: and particularly concerning myself, in what parts of the land, and how long in each, I had dwelt; and after what manner I lived there; and of my age; and in what part or place when GOD sent me home, I should take up my abode? To all which, I gave answers.

They desired to know also, how many Englishmen there were yet remaining behind. I gave them an account of sixteen men, and also of eighteen children born there.

They much inquired concerning their Ambassadors detained there, and of their behaviour and manner of living; also what the King allowed them for maintenance; and concerning several officers of quality, prisoners there; and in general, about all the rest of their nation.

And what "countenance the King showed to those Dutchmen that came running away to him?" I answered, "The Dutch runaways, the King looks upon as rogues."

And concerning the Portuguese, they inquired also. I told them, "The Portuguese were about some fifty or threescore persons: and six or seven of those, were European born."

They asked moreover, "How we had made our escape? and which way? and by what towns we passed? and how long we were in our journey?" To all which I answered at large.

Then the Governor asked me "What was my intent and desire?" I told him, "To have passage to our own nation at Fort Saint George."

To which he answered, "That suddenly [*immediately*] there

would be no convenient opportunity: but his desire was that we would go with him to Batavia; where the General his father, would be very glad to see us." Which it was not in our power to deny.

Then he commanded to call a Dutch Captain; who was over the countries adjacent, subject to their jurisdiction. To whom he gave orders to take us home to his house, and there well to entertain us, and also to send for a tailor to make us clothes.

Upon which I told him: "That his kindness shown us already, was more than we could have desired. It would be a sufficient favour now to supply us with a little money upon a bill to be paid at Fort Saint George, that we might therewith clothe ourselves."

To which he answered, "That he would not deny me any sum I should demand, and clothe us upon his own account besides." For which, we humbly thanked his Lordship: and so took our leave of him; and went home with the aforesaid Captain.

The Governor presently sent me money by his steward for expenses when we walked abroad in the city.

We were nobly entertained without lack of anything all the time we stayed at Colombo. My consort's ague increased, and grew very bad; but the Chief Surgeon, by order, daily came to see him; and gave him such potions of physic, that by GOD's blessing, he soon after recovered.

During my being here, I wrote a letter to my fellow-prisoners that I left behind me in Kandy: wherein I described, at large, the way we went, so that they might plainly understand the same; which I finding to be safe and secure, advised them when GOD permitted, to steer the same course. This letter I left with the new Governor of Colombo and desired him, when opportunity presented, to send it to them: who said he would have it copied out into Dutch, for the benefit of their prisoners there; and promised to send both together.

The Governor seemed to be pleased with my aforesaid relations and replies to his demands; insomuch that he afterwards appointed one that well understood Portuguese to write down all the former particulars. Which being done; for further satisfaction, they brought me pen and paper, desiring me to write the same, that I had related to them, in English and to sign it with my hand: which I was not unwilling to do.

Upon the Governor's departure, there were great and royal feasts made: to which he always sent for me. Here were exceeding great varieties of food, wine and sweetmeats; and music.

Some two and twenty days after our arrival at Colombo, the Governor went on board ship to sail to Batavia; and took us with him. At which time there were many scores of ordnance fired.

We sailed all the day with flag and pennant under it; being out both day and night; in a ship of about 800 tons burden; and a soldier standing armed as a sentinel at the cabin door, both night and day. The Governor so far favoured me that I was in his own mess, and eat at his table; where every meal, we had ten or twelve dishes of meat, with variety of wine.

We set sail from Colombo the 24th of November; and the 5th of January [1680] anchored in Batavia road.

As we came to greater men, so we found greater kindness: for the General of Batavia's reception of us and favours to us, exceeded if possible, those of the Governor his son. As soon as we came before him; seeming to be very glad, he took me by the hand and bade me "heartily welcome, thanking GOD on our behalf, that had appeared so miraculously in our deliverance;" telling us withal, "that he had omitted no means for our redemption; and that if it had been in his power, we should long before have had our liberty."

I humbly thanked his Excellency, and said, "That I knew it to be true; and that though it missed of an effect, yet his good will was not the less, neither were our obligations; being ever bound to thank and pray for him."

Then his own tailor was ordered to take measure of us, and to furnish us with two suits of apparel. He gave us also money for tobacco and betel, and to spend in the city. All the time we stayed there, our quarters were in the Captain of the Castle's house. And oftentimes the General would send for me to his own table, at which sat only himself and his lady who was all bespangled with diamonds and pearls. Sometimes his sons and daughters-in-law, with some other strangers did eat with him: the trumpets sounding all the while.

We finding ourselves thus kindly entertained, and our habits changed; saw that we were no more captives in Kandy, nor yet prisoners elsewhere: therefore we cut off our beards which we had brought with us out of our captivity (for until then, we cut them not); GOD having rolled away the reproach of Kandy from us.

Here also, they did examine me again, concerning the passages of Kandy; causing all to be written down which I said, and requiring my hand to the same: which I refused as I had done before, and upon the same account—because I understood not the Dutch language. Whereupon they persuaded me to write a certificate upon another paper under my hand, that what I had informed them of was true. Which I did. This examination was taken by two secretaries, who were appointed to demand answers of me concerning the King of Ceylon and his country: which they committed to writing from my mouth.

The General's youngest son being to go home Admiral of the ships this year, the General kindly offered us passage upon their ships; promising me entertainment at his son's own table, as the Governor of Colombo had given me in my voyage thither: which offer he made me, he said, "that I might better satisfy their Company in Holland concerning the affairs of Ceylon; which they would be very glad to know."

At this time came two English merchants hither from Bantam: with whom the General was pleased to permit us to go.

But when we came to Bantam, the English Agent [of the English East India Company] very kindly entertained us; and being not willing that we should go to the Dutch for a passage, since GOD had brought us to our own nation, ordered our passage in the good ship *Cæsar* lying then in the road, for England the land of our nativity and our long wished for port. Where by the good providence of GOD, we arrived safe in the month of September [1680].

CHAPTER XIII.

Concerning some other nations, and chiefly European that now live in the island. The Portuguese and Dutch.

HAVING SAID all this concerning the English people, it may not be unacceptable to give some account of other whites, who either voluntarily or by constraint inhabit there: and they are besides the English already spoken of; Portuguese, Dutch and French.

But before I enter upon a discourse of any of these, I shall detain my readers a little with another nation inhabiting this land, I mean the Malabars: both because they are strangers and derive themselves from another country; and also because I have had occasion to mention them sometimes in this book.

These Malabars, then, are voluntary inhabitants of the island; and have a country here, though the limits of it are but small. It lies to the northward of the King's coasts, betwixt him and the Hollanders. Corunda Oya parts it from the King's territories. Through this country we passed, when we made our escape. The language they speak is peculiar to themselves; so that a Cingalese cannot understand them, nor they a Cingalese.

They have a Prince over them, called *Coilat Wannea*, that is independent both of the King of Kandy on the one hand, and of the Dutch on the other: only that he pays an acknowledgment to the Hollanders, who have endeavoured to subdue him by wars, but they cannot yet do it. Yet they have brought him to be a tributary to them, viz.: to pay a certain rate of elephants *per annum*. The King and this Prince maintain a friendship and correspondence together: and when the King lately sent an army against the Hollanders, this Prince let them pass through his country; and went himself in person, to direct the King's people; when they took one or two forts from them.

The people are in great subjection under him. They pay him rather greater taxes than the Cingalese do to their King: but he is nothing so cruel. He victualleth his soldiers during the time they are upon the guard, either about the palace or abroad in the wars: whereas it is the contrary in the King's country; for the Cingalese soldiers bear their own expenses. He hath a certain rate out of every land that is sown; which is to maintain his charge.

The commodities of this country are elephants, honey, butter, milk, wax, cows, wild cattle; of the last three, a great abundance. As for corn, it is more scarce than in the Cingalese country; neither have they any cotton: but they come up into Nuwerakalawe yearly, with great droves of cattle; and lade back both corn and cotton. And to buy these they bring up cloth made of the same cotton, which they can make better than the Cingalese; also they bring salt, and salt fish, brass basins, and other commodities; which they get of the Hollander. Because the King permits not his people to have any manner of trade with the Hollander; so they receive the Dutch commodities at second hand.

We will now proceed unto the European nations: and we will begin with the Portuguese; who deserve the first place; being the oldest standers there.

The sea-coasts round about the island were formerly under their power and government: and so held for many years. In which time, many of the natives became Christians, and learned the Portuguese tongue; which to this day is much spoken in that land, for even the King himself understands and speaks it excellently well.

The Portuguese have often made invasions throughout the whole land, even to Kandy the metropolis of the island; which they have burnt more than once with the palace and the temples. And so formidable have they been that the King hath been forced to turn tributary to them, paying them three elephants *per annum*. However the middle of the island, viz., Conde Uda, standing upon mountains, and so strongly fortified by nature; could never be brought into subjection by them, much less by any other: but hath always been under the power of their own kings.

There were great and long wars between the King of

Ceylon and the Portuguese; and many of the brave Portuguese generals are still in memory among them: of whom I shall relate some passages presently. Great vexation they gave the King by their irruptions into his dominions, and the mischiefs they did him; though oftentimes with great loss on their side. Great battles have been lost and won between them; with great destruction of men on both parts. But being greatly distressed at last; he sent and called in the Hollander to his aid: by whose seasonable assistance, together with his own arms; the King totally dispossessed the Portuguese and routed them out of the land. Whose room the Dutch now occupy; paying themselves for their pains.

At the surrender of Colombo, which was the last place the Portuguese held, the King made a proclamation, that all Portuguese which would come unto him, should be well entertained: which accordingly many did, with their whole families, wives, children and servants; choosing rather to be under him than the Dutch. And divers of them are alive to this day, living in Conde Uda; and others are born there. To all of whom, he alloweth monthly maintenance, yea also and provisions for their slaves and servants which they brought up with them. These people are privileged to travel the countries above all other whites, as knowing they will not run away. Also when there was a trade at the seaports; they were permitted to go down with commodities, clear from all customs and duties.

Besides those who came voluntarily to live under the King: there are others whom he took prisoners. The Portuguese of the best quality, the King took into his service: who have been, most of them, since cut off; according to his kind custom towards his courtiers. The rest of them have an allowance from the King; and follow husbandry, trading about the country, distilling arrack, keeping taverns; or the women sew women's waistcoats, and the men sew men's doublets for sale.

I shall now mention some of the last Portuguese generals, all within the present King's reign; with some passages concerning them.

CONSTANTINE SA, General of the Portuguese army in Ceylon when the Portuguese had footing in this land, was very successful against this present King. He ran quite through the island unto the royal city itself; which he set on fire, with the temples therein. Insomuch that the King sent a message to him signifying that he was willing to become his tributary. But he proudly sent him word back again, "That that would not serve his turn: he should not only be tributary but slave to his master, the King of Portugal." This, the King of Kandy could not brook, being of an high stomach; and said, "He would fight to the last drop of blood, rather than stoop to that."

There were at this time, many commanders in the General's army, who were natural Cingalese: with these, the King dealt secretly; assuring them that if they would turn on his side, he would gratify them with very ample rewards. The King's promises took effect; and they all revolted from the General. The King now — not daring to trust the revolted to make trial of their truth and fidelity—put them in the forefront of his battle; and commanded them to give the first onset. The King at that time, might have had 20,000 or 30,000 men in the field: who, taking their opportunity, set upon the Portuguese army and gave them such a total overthrow; that, as they report in that country, not one of them escaped. The General seeing his defeat, and himself likely to be taken; called his black boy to give him water to drink; and snatching the knife that stuck by his boy's side, stabbed himself with it.

Another General after him, was LEWIS TISSÉRA. He swore that he would make the King eat *coracan tallipa*, that is, a kind of hasty pudding made of water and the coracan flour, which is reckoned the worst fare of that island. The King afterwards took this LEWIS TISSÉRA; and put him in chains in the common gaol, and made him eat of the same fare. And there is a ballad of this man and this passage, sung much among the common people there to this day.

Their next General was SIMON CAREE, a natural Cingalese, but baptized. He is said to have been a great commander. When he had got any victory over the Cingalese, he did exercise great cruelty. He would make the women beat their own children to pieces in their mortars; wherein they used to beat their corn.

GASPAR FIGARI had a Portuguese father and a Cingalese

mother. He was the last general they had in this country, and a brave soldier: but degenerated not from his predecessors in cruelty. He would hang up the people by the heels, and split them down the middle. He had his axe wrapped in a white cloth, which he carried with him into the field, to execute those he suspected to be false to him or that attempted to run away. Smaller malefactors he was merciful to, cutting off only their right hands. Several whom he hath so served are yet living, whom I have seen.

This GASPAR came up one day to fight against the King: and the King resolved to fight him. The General fixed his camp at Motaupul in Hotterakorle. And in order to the King's coming down to meet the Portuguese, preparation was made for him at a place called Catta coppul, which might be ten or twelve miles distant from the Portuguese army. GASPAR knew of the place by some spies, but of the time of the King's coming he was informed that it was a day sooner than really it happened. According to this information, he resolved privately to march thither; and come upon him in the night unawares. And because he knew the King was a politician, and would have his spies abroad to watch the General's motion; the General sent for all the drummers and pipers to play and dance in his camp that thereby the King's spies might not suspect that he was upon the march, but merry and secure in his camp.

In the meantime, having set his people all to their dancing and drumming, he left a small party there to secure the baggage; and away he goes in the night with his army, and arrives at Catta coppul, intending to fall upon the King. But when he came thither, he found the King was not yet come; but into the King's tent he went, and sate him down in the seat appointed for the King. Here he heard where the King was with his camp; which being not far off, he marched thither in the morning, and fell upon him; and gave him one of the greatest routs that ever he had.

The King himself had a narrow escape. For had it not been for a Dutch company, which the Dutch had sent a little before for his guard: who, after his own army fled, turned head and stopped the Portuguese for a while; he had been seized. The Portuguese General was so near the King, that he called after him, *Houre*, that is "Brother, Stay! I would speak with you!" But the King having got atop of the hills, was safe: and so GASPAR retired to his quarters.

This gallant expert Commander, that had so often vanquished the Cingalese; could not cope with another European nation. For when the Hollanders came to besiege Colombo, he was sent against them with his army. They told him before he went, that now he must look to himself: for he was not now to fight against Cingalese; but against soldiers that would look him in the face. But he made nothing of them, and said that he would serve them as he had served the Cingalese. The Hollanders met him, and they fought; but they had before contrived a stratagem, which he was not aware of. They had placed some field-pieces in the rear of their army; and after a small skirmish, they retreated as if they had been worsted, which was only to draw the Portuguese nearer upon their guns: which, when they had brought them in shot of, they opened on a sudden to the right and left, and fired upon them; and so routed them, and drove them into Colombo.

This GASPAR was in the city, when it was taken; and was himself taken prisoner: who was afterwards sent to Goa; where he died.

And so much of the Portuguese.

The Dutch succeeded the Portuguese. The first occasion of whose coming into this land was that the present King, being wearied and overmatched with the Portuguese, sent for them into his aid long ago from Batavia. And they did him good service; but they feathered their own nests by the means; and are now possessed of all the sea-coasts, and considerable territories thereunto adjoining.

The King of the country keeps up an irreconcilable war against them: the occasion of which is said to have been this.

Upon the besieging of Colombo, which was about the year 1655: it was concluded upon between the King and the Dutch, that their enemies the Portuguese being expelled thence; the city was to be delivered up by the Dutch into the King's hands. Whereupon the King himself in person, with all his power; went down to this war, to assist and and join with the Hollanders: without whose help, as it is generally reported, the Dutch could not have taken the city.

But being surrendered to them, and they gotten into it; the King lay looking for when they would come, according to their former articles, and put him into possession of it. Meanwhile they turned on a sudden, and fell upon him, contrary to his expectation—whether the King had first broke word with them is not known—and took bag and baggage from him. Which provoked him in so high a manner, that he maintains a constant hostility against them; detains their Ambassadors; and forbids his people, upon pain of death, to hold commerce with them.

So that the Dutch have enough to do to maintain those places which they have. Oftentimes the King, at unawares falls upon them and does them great spoil: sometimes giving no quarter, but cutting off the heads of whomsoever he catches: which are brought up and hung upon trees near the city; many of which I have seen. Sometimes he brings up his prisoners alive and keeps them by the highway sides, a spectacle to the people in memory of his victories over them. Many of these are now living there in a most miserable condition, having but a very small allowance from him; so that they are forced to beg, and it is a favour when they can get leave to go abroad and do it.

The Dutch, therefore, not being able to deal with him by the sword, being unacquainted with the woods and the Cingalese manner of fighting; do endeavour for peace with him all they can: dispatching divers Ambassadors to him, and sending great presents; by carrying letters to him in great state, wrapped up in silks wrought with gold and silver; bearing them all the way upon their heads, in token of great honour; honouring him with great and high titles; subscribing themselves his subjects and servants; telling him that the forts they build, are out of loyalty to him, to secure His Majesty's country from foreign enemies; and that when they came up into his country, it was to seek maintenance.

And by these flatteries and submissions, they sometimes obtain to keep what they have gotten from him; and sometimes nothing will prevail: he, neither regarding their Ambassadors nor receiving the presents; but taking his opportunity upon a sudden, of setting on them with his forces.

His craft and success in taking Belligam fort, in the county of Habberagon; may deserve to be mentioned. The Cingalese had besieged the fort, and knowing the Dutch had no water there, but that all they had was conveyed through a trench wrought under ground from a river near by: they besieged them so closely and planted so many guns towards the mouth of this trench; that they could not come out to fetch water. They cut down wood also, and made bundles of faggots therewith: which they piled up around about the fort at some distance; and every night removed them nearer and nearer: so their works became higher than the fort. Their main intent by these faggot-works, was to have brought them just under the fort, and then to have set it on fire: the walls of the fort being for the most part of wood. There was also a boabab tree growing just by the fort; on which they planted guns, and shot right down into them. The houses in the fort being thatched; they shot also fire arrows among them: so that the besieged were forced to pull off the straw from their houses, which proved a great inconvenience to them, it being a rainy season; so that they lay open to the weather and cold.

The Dutch finding themselves in this extremity, desired quarter: which was granted them at the King's mercy. They came out and laid down their arms; all but the officers, who still wore theirs. None were plundered of anything they had about them. The fort, the Cingalese demolished to the ground; and brought up the four guns to the King's palace: where they, among others, stand; mounted on broad carriages, before his gate.

The Dutch were brought two or three days' journey from the fort into the country they called Oowah; and there were placed with a guard about them: having but a small allowance appointed them; insomuch that afterwards having spent what they had; they perished for hunger. So that of about ninety Hollanders taken prisoners; there were not above five and twenty living when I came away.

There are several white Ambassadors, besides other Cingalese people, by whom the Dutch have sent letters and presents to the King: whom he keeps from returning back again. They are all bestowed in several houses, with soldiers to guard them. And though they are not in chains; yet none is permitted to come to them or speak with them. It not being the custom of that land for any to come to the speech of Ambassadors. Their allowance is brought them ready dressed out of the King's palace; being of all sorts and varieties that the land affords.

After they have remained in this condition some years, the guards are somewhat slackened and the soldiers that are to watch them grow remiss in their duty; so that now the Ambassadors walk about the streets, and anybody goes to their houses and talks with them: that is after they have been so long in the country, that all their news is stale and grown out of date. But this liberty is only winked at, not allowed.

When they have been there a great while, the King usually gives them slaves, both men and women: the more to alienate their minds from their own country; and that they may stay with him, with the more willingness and content. For his design is to make them, if he can, inclinable to serve him: as he prevailed with one of these Ambassadors to do for the love of a woman. The manner of it I shall relate immediately.

There were five Ambassadors whom he hath thus detained, since my coming there; of each of whom, I shall speak a little: besides two, whom he sent away voluntarily.

The first of these was sent up by the Hollanders, some time before the rebellion against the King [in 1664]; who detained him in the city. After the rebellion, the King sent for him to him to the mountain of Gauluda; whither he had retreated from the rebels. The King not long after removed to Digligy, where he now keeps his Court: but left the Ambassador at Gauluda remaining by himself, with a guard of soldiers. In this uncomfortable condition, upon a dismal mountain, void of all society; he continued many days. During which time, a Cingalese and his wife fell out, and she being discontented with her husband, to escape from him flies to this Ambassador's house for shelter. The woman being somewhat beautiful; he fell greatly in love with her: and to obtain her, he sent to the King and proffered him his service if he would permit him to enjoy her company. Which the King was very willing and glad to do, having now obtained that which he had long aimed at, to get him into his service.

Hereupon the King sent him word that he granted his desire, and withal sent to both of them rich apparel; and to her, many jewels and bracelets of gold and silver.

Suddenly afterwards there was a great house prepared for them in the city, furnished with all kind of furniture out of the King's treasure, and at his proper cost and charges. Which being finished, he was brought away from his mountain, into it: but from thenceforward he never saw his wife more, according to the custom of the Court. And he was entertained in the King's service, and made *Courtalbad*, which is Chief over all the smiths and carpenters in Conde Uda.

Some short time after, the King about to send his forces against a fort of the Hollanders called Arranderre, built by them in the year 1666; he, though in the King's service, yet being a well-wisher to his country, had privately sent a letter of advice to the Dutch concerning the King's intention and purpose; an answer to which was intercepted, and brought to the King; wherein "thanks were returned to him from the Dutch for his loyalty to his own nation, and that they would accordingly prepare for the King's assault."

The King having read this letter, sent for him, and bade him read it; which he excused, pretending it was so written that he could not. Whereupon immediately another Dutchman was sent for; who read it before the King, and told him the contents of it. At which it is reported that the King said *Beia pas mettandi hitta pas ettandi*, that is, "He serves me for fear, and them for love," or "His fear is here, and his love there:" and forthwith commanded to carry him forth to execution; which was accordingly done upon him. It is generally said that this letter was framed by somebody on purpose to ruin him.

The next Ambassador after him was HENDRICK DRAAK, a fine gentleman, and a good friend of the English. This was he who was commissioned in the year 1664 to intercede with the King on behalf of the English, that they might have liberty to go home; and with him they were made to believe they should return: which happened at the same time that Sir EDWARD WINTER sent his letters to the King for us; which I have already spoken of in the Fifth Chapter of this Fourth Part.

This Ambassador was much in the King's favour, with whom he was detained till he died. And then the King sent his body down to Colombo, carried in a palankin with great state and lamentation; and accompanied with his great commanders and many soldiers.

Some time after the loss of the fort of Arranderre, which was about the year 1670: the Dutch sent up another Ambassador to see if he could obtain peace: which was the first time their Ambassadors began to bring up letters upon their heads in token of extraordinary reverence. This man was much favoured by the King, and was entertained with great ceremony and honour: he clothing him in Cingalese habit, which I never knew done before nor since. But being weary of his long stay, and of the delays that were made; having often made motions to go down to the coast and still he was deferred from day to day: at length he made a resolution, that if he had not leave by such a day, he would go without it; saying "the former ambassador [H. DRAAK], who died there, died like a woman; but it should be seen that he would die like a man."

At the appointed day, he girt on his sword, and repaired to the gates of the King's palace; pulling off his hat, and making his obeisance, as if the King were present before him: and thanking him for the favours and honours he had done him; and so took his leave. And there being some Englishmen present, he generously gave them some money to drink his health: and in this resolute manner departed, with some two or three black servants that attended on him. The upshot of which was, that the King, not being willing to prevent his resolution by violence, sent one of his noblemen to conduct him down: and so he had the good fortune to get home safely to Colombo.

The next Ambassador after him, was JOHN BAPTISTA: a man of a milder spirit than the former; endeavouring to please and show compliance with the King. He obtained many favours of the King, and several slaves, both men and women: and living well, with servants about him; is the more patient in waiting the King's leisure, till he pleaseth to send him home.

The last Ambassador that came up while I was there, brought up a lion; which the Dutch thought would be the most acceptable present that they could send to the King; as indeed did all others. It was but a whelp. But the King did never receive it, supposing it not so famous as he had heard by report lions were. This man with his lion was brought up and kept in the county of Ooddaboolat, nearly twenty miles from the King's Court: where he remained about a year; in the which time the lion died.

The Ambassador, being weary of living thus like a prisoner, with a guard always upon him, often attempted to go back; seeing the King would not permit him audience: but the guards would not let him. Having divers times made disturbances in this manner to get away home; the King commanded to bring him up into the city to an house that was prepared for him, standing some distance from the Court. Where having waited many days, and seeing no signs of audience; he resolved to make his appearance before the King by force: which he attempted to do; when the King was abroad taking his pleasure. The soldiers of his guard immediately ran, and acquainted the noblemen at Court of his coming; who delayed not to acquaint the King thereof. Whereupon the King gave order forthwith to meet him; and where they met him in that same place to stop him till further orders. And there they kept him, not letting him go either forward or backward. In this manner and place, he remained for three days: till the King sent orders that he might return to his house whence he came. This the King did to tame him. But afterwards he was pleased to call him before him. And there he remained when I left the country; maintained with plenty of provisions at the King's charge.

The number of Dutch now living there may be about fifty or sixty. Some whereof are Ambassadors; some prisoners of war; some runaways and malefactors that have escaped the hand of justice, and got away from the Dutch quarters. To all of whom, are allotted respective allowances; but the runaways have the least, the King not loving such, though giving them entertainment.

The Dutch here love drink, and so practise their proper vice in this country. One who was a great man in the Court, would sometime come into the King's presence, half disguised with drink; which the King often passed over: but once asked him, "Why do you thus disorder yourself that when I send for you about my business, you are not in a capacity to serve me?" He boldly replied, "That as soon as his mother took away her milk from him; she supplied it with wine: and ever since," saith he, "I have used myself to it," With this answer, the King seemed to be pleased. And indeed the rest of the white men are generally of the same temper; insomuch that the Cingalese have a saying, "That wine is as natural to white men as milk to children."

All differences of ranks and qualities are disregarded among those Cingalese people that are under the Dutch. Neither do the Dutch make any distinction between the "Hondrews," and the low and inferior castes of men; and permit them to go in the same habit, and sit upon stools, as well as the best Hondrews: and the lower ranks may eat and intermarry with the higher without any punishment or any cognizance taken of it. Which is a matter that the Cingalese in Conde Uda are much offended with the Dutch for; and makes them think, that they themselves are sprung from some mean rank or extract. And this prejudiceth this people against them; that they have not such an esteem for them. For to a Cingalese, his rank and honour is as dear as his life.

And thus much of the Dutch.

CHAPTER XIV.

Concerning the French. With some inquiries what should make the King detain white men as he does. And how the Christian religion is maintained among the Christians there.

ABOUT the year 1672 or 1673; there came fourteen sail of great ships from the King of France to settle a trade here. Monsieur DE LA HAYE the Admiral, put in with his fleet into the port of Kottiaar. From whence, he sent up three men by way of embassy, to the King of Kandy: whom he entertained very nobly, and gave every one of them a chain of gold about their necks, and a sword all inlaid with silver, and a gun. And afterwards he sent one of them down to the Admiral with his answer which encouraged him to send up others, that is, an Ambassador, and six more, who were to reside there, till the return of the fleet back again; the fleet being about to sail to the coast of Coromandel.

To the fleet, the King sent all manner of provisions, as much as his ability could afford; and not only permitted but assisted them to build a fort in the bay: which they manned, partly with their own people and partly with Cingalese, whom the king sent and lent to the French. But the Admiral finding that the King's provisions, and what else could be brought in the island, would not suffice for so great a fleet: was forced to depart for the coast of Coromandel, promising the King by the Ambassador aforementioned, speedily to return again. So leaving some of his men with the King's supplies [*auxiliaries*] to keep the fort till his return: he weighed anchor and set sail. But never came back again. Some reported they were destroyed by a storm; others by the Dutch. The Admiral had sent up to the King great presents, but he would not presently receive them; that it might not seem as if he wanted anything or were greedy of things brought to him: but since the French returned not according to their promise; he scorned ever after to receive them. At first, he neglected the present out of State; and ever since out of anger and indignation. The French fort at Kottiaar was a little after, easily taken by the Dutch.

But to return to the Ambassador and his retinue. He rode up from Kottiaar on horseback; which was very grand in that country: and being, with his company, gotten somewhat short of the city [of Digligy], was appointed there to stay until an house should be prepared in the city for their entertainment. When it was signified to him that their house was ready for their reception; they were conducted forward by certain nobleman sent by the King, carrying with them a present for his majesty. The Ambassador came riding on horseback into the city, which the noblemen observing, dissuaded him from, and advised him to walk on foot; telling him it was not allowable nor the custom: but he, regarding them not, rode by the palace gate. It offended the King; but he took not much notice of it for the present.

The Ambassador alighted at his lodgings, where he and his companions were nobly entertained; and provisions sent them ready dressed out of the King's palace three times a day. Great plenty they had of all things the country afforded.

After some time, the King sent to him to come to his audience. In great state, he was conducted to the Court; accompanied with several of the nobles that were sent to him. Coming—thus to the Court in the night—as it is the King's usual manner at that season [*time*] to send for foreign ministers, and give them audience—he waited there some small time about two hours or less, the King not yet admitting him. Which he took in such great disdain, and for such an affront that he was made to stay at all; much more so long: that he would tarry no longer but went towards his lodgings. Some about the Court observing this, would have stopped him by elephants that stood in the court, turning them before the gate, through which he was to pass: but he would not so be stopped, but laid his hand upon his sword, as if he meant to make his way by the elephants. The people seeing his resolution, called away the elephants, and let him pass.

As soon as the King heard of it, he was highly displeased; insomuch that he commanded some of his officers, that they should go, and beat them and clap them in chains: which was immediately done to all; excepting the two gentlemen that were first sent up by the Admiral. (For these were not touched, the King reckoning they did not belong unto this Ambassador: neither were they now in his company; excepting that one of them in the combustion got a few blows.) They were likewise disarmed, and so have continued ever since. Upon this the gentlemen, attendants upon the Ambassador, made their complaints to the captain of their guards; excusing themselves and laying all the blame upon their Ambassador: urging "that they were his attendants, and a soldier must obey his commander, and go where he appoints him." Which sayings being told the King, he approved thereof, and commanded them out of chains: the Ambassador still remaining in them, and so continued for six months. After which, he was released from his chains, by means of the entreaties his own men made to the great men in his behalf.

The rest of the Frenchmen, seeing how the Ambassador's imprudent carriage had brought him to this misery, refused any longer to dwell with him: and each of them by the King's permission dwells by himself in the city; being maintained at the King's charge. Three of these—whose names were Monsieur DU PLESSY, son to a gentleman of note in France; and JEAN BLOOM; the third—whose name I cannot tell, but he was the Ambassador's boy—the King appointed to look to his best horse kept in the palace. This horse some time after died, as it is supposed of old age: which extremely troubled the King. And imagining they had been instrumental in his death, by their carelessness: he commanded two of them, Monsieur DU PLESSY and JEAN BLOOM, to be carried away into the mountains, and kept prisoners in chains. Where they remained when I came thence.

The rest of them follow employments: some whereof distil arrack, and keep the greatest taverns in the city.

Lately—a little before I came from the island—the King understanding the disagreements and differences that were still kept on foot betwixt the Ambassador and the rest of his company, disliked it; and used these means to make them friends. He sent for them all, the Ambassador and the rest; and told them, "that it was not seemly for persons as they were, at such a distance from their own country, to quarrel and fall out; and that if they had any love for GOD or the King of France or himself; they should go home with the Ambassador and agree and live together." They went back together not daring to disobey the King: and as soon as they were at home, the King sent a banquet after them of sweetmeats and fruits to eat together. They did eat the King's banquet; but it would not make the reconcilement. For after they had done, each man went home; and dwelt in their own houses, as they did before. It was thought that this carriage would offend the King, and that he would, at least, take away their allowance: and it is probable, before this time the King hath taken vengeance on them. But the Ambassador's carriage is so imperious, that they would rather venture whatsoever might follow than be subject to him. And in this case I left them.

Since my return to England; I presumed by a letter to inform the French Ambassador then in London of the aforesaid matters: thinking myself bound in conscience and Christian charity to do my endeavour; that their friends knowing their condition, may use means for their deliverance. The letter ran thus.

"*These may acquaint your Excellency, that having been a prisoner in the island of Ceylon, under the King of that country nearly twenty years: by means of this my long detainment there, I became acquainted with the French Ambassador and the other gentlemen of his retinue, being in all eight persons; who were sent to treat with the said King in the year 1672, by Monsieur* DE LA HAYE*; who came with a fleet to the port of Kottiaar or Trincomalee, from whence he sent these gentlemen. And knowing that from thence it is scarcely possible to send any letters or notice to other parts—for in all the time of my captivity, I could never send one word whereby my friends here might come to hear of my condition; until with one more, I made an escape, leaving sixteen Englishmen yet there—the kindness I have received from those French gentlemen, as also my compassion for them being detained in the same place with me: have obliged and constrained me to* *presume to trouble your Lordship with this paper; not knowing any other means whereby I might convey notice to their friends and relations, which is all the service I am able to perform for them.*

"*The Ambassador's name I know not. There is a kinsman of his, called Monsieur* LE SERLE, *and a young gentleman called Monsieur* DU PLESSY, *and another named Monsieur* LA ROCHE. *The rest, by name I know not.*"

And then an account of them is given, according to what I have mentioned above.

"*I shall not presume to be further tedious to your Honour. Craving pardon for my boldness, which an affection to those gentlemen, being in the same land with me, hath occasioned; concerning whom if your Lordship be pleased further to be informed, I shall be both willing and ready to be.*

"*Yours, &c.*"

The Ambassador upon the receipt of this, desired to speak with me. Upon whom I waited, and he, after some speech with me; told me he would send word into France of it, and gave me thanks for this my kindness to his countrymen.

It may be worth some inquiry, what the reason might be, that the King detains the European people as he does. It cannot be out of hope of profit or advantage, for they are so far from bringing him any, that they are a very great charge; being all maintained either by him or his people. Neither is it in the power of money to redeem any one; for that he neither needs nor values. Which makes me conclude it is not out of profit or envy or ill-will, but out of love and favour, that he keeps them; delighting in their company, and to have them ready at his command.

For he is very ambitious of the service of these men; and winks at many of their failings, more than he uses to do towards his natural subjects.

As may appear from a Company of white soldiers he hath, who upon their watch used to be very negligent; one lying drunk here, and another there: which remissness in his own soldiers, he would scarcely have endured, but it would have cost their lives; but with these, he useth more craft than severity to make them more watchful.

These soldiers are under two Captains, the one a Dutchman and the other a Portuguese. They are appointed to guard one of the King's magazines; where they always keep sentinel, both by day and night. This is a pretty good distance from the Court, and here it was the King contrived their station, that they might swear and swagger out of his hearing, and that nobody might disturb them nor they nobody. The Dutch captain lies at one side of the gate, and the Portuguese at the other.

Once the King, to employ these his white soldiers, and to honour them, by letting them see what an assurance he reposed in them; sent one of his boys thither to be kept prisoner, which they were very proud of. They kept him two years in which time he had learnt both the Dutch and Portuguese language. Afterwards the King retook the boy into his service; and within a short time after, executed him.

But the King's reason in sending this boy to be kept by these soldiers was probably, not as they supposed and as the king himself outwardly pretended, viz.:—to show how much he confided in them, but out of design to make them look the better to their watch, which their debauchery made them very remiss in. For the prisoner's hands only were in chains, and not his legs. So that his possibility of running away, having his legs at liberty; concerned them to be circumspect and wakeful: and they knew if he had escaped it were as much as their lives were worth. By this crafty and kind way did the king correct the negligence of his white soldiers.

Indeed his inclinations are much towards the Europeans, making them his great officers; accounting them more faithful and trusty than his own people. With these he often discourses concerning the affairs of their countries, and promotes to places far above their ability and sometimes their degree or desert. And indeed all over the land they do bear, as it were, a natural respect and reverence to white men; inasmuch as black, they hold to be inferior to white: and they say the gods are white, and that the souls of the blessed after the resurrection will be white; and therefore that black is a rejected and accursed colour.

And as further signs of the King's favour to them, there are many privileges which the white men have and enjoy, as tolerated or allowed them from the King, which I suppose may proceed from the aforesaid consideration: as, to wear any manner of apparel, either gold, silver or silk, shoes and stockings, a shoulder belt and sword; their houses may be whitened with lime; and many such things: all which the Cingalese are not permitted to do.

He will also sometimes send for them into his presence, and discourse familiarly with them, and entertain them with great civilities; especially white Ambassadors. They are greatly chargeable unto his country, but he regards it not in the least. So that the people are more like slaves unto us, than we to the King: inasmuch as they are enforced by his command to bring us maintenance. Whose poverty is so great oftentimes, that for want of what they supply us with; themselves, their wives and children are forced to suffer hunger. This being as a due tax imposed upon them to pay unto us. Neither can they by any power or authority refuse the payment thereof to us. For in my own hearing, the people once complaining of their poverty and inability to give us any longer our allowance, the magistrate or governor replied, "It was the King's special command, and who durst disannul it? And if otherwise they could not supply us with our maintenance; he bade them sell their wives and children, rather than we should want of our due." Such is the favour that Almighty GOD hath given Christian people in the sight of this heathen King; whose entertainment and usage of them is thus favourable.

If any inquire into the religious exercise and worship practised among the Christians there: I am sorry I must say it; I can give but a slender account. For they have no churches, nor no priests; and so no meetings together on the Lord's days for Divine Worship; but each one reads and prays at his own house, as he is disposed. They sanctify the day chiefly by refraining work, and meeting together at drinking houses. They continue the practice of baptism. And there being no priests, they baptize their children themselves with water, and use the words "In the name of the FATHER, and of the SON, and of the HOLY GHOST;" and give them Christian names. They have their friends about them at such a time, and make a small feast, according to their ability: and some teach their children to say their prayers, and to read; and some do not.

Indeed their religion, at the best, is but negative, that is, they are not heathen; they do not comply with the idolatry here practised: and they profess themselves Christians in a general manner; which appears by their names, and by their beads and crosses, that some of them wear about their necks.

Nor indeed can I wholly clear them from compliance with the religion of the country. For some of them, when they are sick do use the ceremonies which the heathen do in the like case: as in making idols of clay, and setting them up in their houses, and offering rice to them; and having weavers to dance before them. But they are ashamed to be known to do this: and I have known none to do it, but such as are Indian born. Yet I never knew any of them, that do inwardly in heart and conscience incline to the ways of the heathen; but perfectly abhor them. Nor have there been any, I ever heard of, that came to their temples, upon any religious account; but only would stand by and look on: without it were one old priest, named Padre VERGONSE, a Genoese born and of the Jesuit's order; who would go to the temples and eat with the weavers and other ordinary people, of the sacrifices offered to the idols. But with this apology for himself; "That he ate it as common meat and as GOD's creature; and that it was never the worse for the superstition that had passed upon it."

But however this may reflect upon the Father, another thing may be related for his honour. There happened two priests to fall into the hands of the King, on whom he conferred great honours. For having laid aside their habits, they kept about his person; and were the greatest favourites at Court. The King, one day, sent for VERGONSE, and asked him if it would not be better for him to lay aside his old coat and cap; and to do as the other two priests had done, and receive honour from him. He replied to the King, "That he boasted more in that old habit, and in the name of JESUS; than in all the honour that he could do him." And so refused the King's honour. The King valued the Father for this saying.

He had a pretty library about him, and died in his bed of old age: whereas the two other priests in the King's service, died miserably; one of a cancer, and the other was slain.

The old priest had about thirty or forty books; which the king, they say, seized on after his death, and keeps.

These priests and more, lived there; but were all deceased, excepting VERGONSE, before my time. The King allowed them to build a church. Which they did, and the Portuguese assembled there. But they made no better than a bawdy house of it. For which cause, the King commanded to pull it down.

Although here be Protestants and Papists, yet here are no differences kept up among them; but they are as good friends as if there were no such parties: and there is no other distinction of religion there, but only heathens and Christians; and we usually say, "We Christians."

FINIS.

Curiously enough, the name of this native King does not transpire in the above narrative. It was Rajah SINGHA the Second. He lived till 1687.

The names of places in the original work have been corrected by those in that most valuable Map of Ceylon, by Major-General JOHN FRASER.